D1400360

WE KNEW

Stonewall Jackson

Richard Wheeler

Thomas Y. Crowell Company
New York
Established 1834

Designed by Leslie Phillips

Manufactured in the United States of America

Library of Congress Cataloging in Publication Data

Wheeler, Richard.
  We knew Stonewall Jackson.

  Bibliography: p.
  Includes index.
  SUMMARY: A biography of the great Civil War general which includes many accounts by people who knew him.
  1. Jackson, Thomas Jonathan, 1824–1863. 2. Confederate States of America. Army—Biography. 3. Generals—Confederate States of America—Biography. [1. Jackson, Thomas Jonathan, 1824–1863. 2. Confederate States of America. Army—Biography. 3. Generals—Confederate States of America] I. Title.
E467.1.J15W37 1977   973.7'3'0924 [B] [92] 76-58009
ISBN 0-690-01218-7

1   2   3   4   5   6   7   8   9   10

Other Crowell Books by Richard Wheeler

Voices of 1776
Voices of the Civil War

Preface

While researching his recent book *Voices of the Civil War,* the author came upon many writings—books, pamphlets, magazine articles, news items, and letters—by people who had known Stonewall Jackson. In the present book, these have been brought together to present an eye-witness account of Jackson's life. Many of the contributions are from sources long out of print, some now quite rare. The book's illustrations are by artists and engravers of Jackson's time.

Contents

Illustrations

Maps

We Knew
STONEWALL JACKSON

~I.

West Point and Mexico

~ *Thomas Jackson was born in Clarksburg, western Virginia (later West Virginia), on January 21, 1824. His Scotch-Irish ancestors had arrived in the region as pioneers some fifty years earlier, when the Indians were still disputing the white man's encroachments. The country was tamer now, but still heavily forested and only thinly populated, with Clarksburg itself as yet but a village. The people had retained the self-reliance of their forebears.*

Thomas's father died when he was two years old, and his mother died when he was seven. He and a ten-year-old brother and a five-year-old sister, left penniless, were taken in by families of relatives. Thomas was raised by an amiable uncle, Cummins Jackson, on a farm near Weston, about twenty miles south of his birthplace. He wasn't blessed with hearty health, but his complaints were more bothersome than serious. They included a form of nervous indigestion that was to be with him for life.

The boy wasn't prevented from living with normal vigor. Exercise, in fact, helped keep his ills at bay. His activities were remarkably varied. Working with his uncle's slaves and hired hands, he helped to raise the farm's crops and livestock; he sheared sheep and processed flax, thus having a hand in the manufacture of some of his own clothing; he learned to make sugar from maple sap; he helped to run his uncle's gristmill and sawmill, and he also worked with the lumbermen in the forest.

He learned something of surveying as an assistant with a crew that

1

routed a new turnpike through the county; he hunted, fished, and trapped; and he became a good horseman, even serving as his uncle's jockey in local races.

"If a horse had any winning qualities whatever in him," a neighbor said later, "Tom Jackson never failed to bring them out."

On the cultural side, Tom took up the violin. He managed to achieve a certain proficiency but never any expertise. He liked to read, often doing so while sitting in the grass by the millrace. One of his favorite books was a romanticized biography of Francis Marion, the "Swamp Fox" of the American Revolution, written by Parson Weems.

The boy's schooling was meager, since the region was short of teachers, but his exposure was sufficient for him to decide that education was the key to both personal and material improvement.

A distant cousin, William E. Arnold, recalled in afteryears:

He was a youth of exemplary habits, of indomitable will and undoubted courage. He was not what is nowadays termed brilliant, but he was one of those untiring, matter-of-fact persons who would never give up an undertaking until he accomplished his object. He learned slowly, but what he got into his head he never forgot. He was not quick to decide, except when excited, and then, when he made up his mind to do a thing, he did it on short notice and in quick time.

Once, while on his way to school, an overgrown rustic behaved rudely to one of the schoolgirls. Jackson fired up and told him he must apologize at once or he would thrash him. The big fellow, supposing that he was more than a match for him, refused, whereupon Jackson pitched into him and gave him a severe pounding.

Ordinarily, says another who knew the boy during these days, "Tom was . . . an uncommonly behaved lad, a gentleman . . . just and kind to everyone."

Tom had a deep sense of morality acquired through his mother and strengthened by contacts with religion. Not committed to a particular church, he attended both Baptist and Methodist services. On several occasions says the daughter of one of Weston's Methodist officials, "Thomas Jackson, a shy, unobtrusive boy, sat with unabated interest in a long sermon, having walked three miles in order to attend."

Tom gained a reputation for integrity. He once made a business

*compact with an area resident, a Conrad Kester, to provide him fresh-
caught fish. When the boy landed an especially large pike one day,
another man offered him the substantial price of a dollar and a quarter
for it.*

*"No," said Tom, "I have an agreement with Mr. Kester to sell him
fish of a certain length for fifty cents each. He has taken some from me a
little shorter. Now he is going to get this big one for fifty cents."*

*At the age of seventeen Tom was made a district constable, a kind of
minor sheriff. Under the date June 11, 1841, a county clerk wrote in
his ledger:*

Thomas Jackson, who was appointed a constable in the 2nd
district . . . this day appeared in open court and entered into
bond . . . and took the several oaths prescribed by law, the court
being of opinion that he is a man of honesty, probity, and good
demeanor.

*Constable Jackson's duties included the serving of notices and the col-
lecting of bad debts. It was not particularly exciting work. A chum
named Sylvanus White—another cousin—imparts a good idea of what
it was like:*

I went with him on one occasion to show him the near way
through the forest, over the hills some three or four miles to a
man's house by the name of Dennis, whom he wished to serve
with a legal process. He left the horse at father's, and we went
on foot. He served the papers, and we returned home.

*There is a better story concerning the young constable's handling of a
man who owed money to a Weston widow. Having been put off several
times, Tom decided to attach the man's horse to force him to make
payment. It was the custom, however, for a horse to be secure from
attachment as long as the owner was in the saddle.*

*One day Tom was standing in front of Weston's livery stable when he
saw the man come riding toward it. Tom stepped back out of sight, then
ran out as the man dismounted. But by the time Tom seized the bridle,
the man had leapt back into the saddle. Disconcerted only for a moment,
Tom led the horse and rider toward a low doorway in the stable, continuing even when lashed by a riding whip. As the doorway was
reached, the man was forced to jump off, and the horse was legally
attached. It was redeemed by a prompt satisfaction of the debt.*

The pay he got as constable was welcome enough, but young Jackson did not like the work. He served for about a year. Then, through his congressman and some influential friends, he won a nomination to the United States Military Academy at West Point. He saw this both as a chance to get a good education and as a step toward an honorable career. The friends who backed him, however, were a little uneasy about his qualifications for the venture.

"I am very ignorant," he told them, "but I can make it up in study."

Jackson reached West Point, on New York's Hudson River, in June 1842. Now eighteen, he was tall, angular, and awkward, with large hands and feet, and his backwoods origins were obvious to the Eastern cadets who noted his arrival. Says Dabney H. Maury, of Fredericksburg, Virginia:

He was clad in gray homespun, and wore a coarse felt hat, such as wagoners or constables—as he had been—usually wore, and bore a pair of weather-stained saddlebags across his shoulders. There was about him so sturdy an expression of purpose that I remarked, "That fellow looks as if he had come to stay."

But Jackson's position was by no means secure. According to Cadet P. T. Turnley, who studied with Jackson:

He had a rough time in the academy at first, for his want of previous training placed him at a great disadvantage, and it was all he could do to pass his first examination.

Not only did Jackson start out in the lowest section of the class (ranking fifty-first among some seventy or eighty), but he was also inept at the military exercises. He could barely keep in step while marching; he was a graceless swordsman, and in spite of his proficiency with horses, he looked ungainly in the saddle.

These things, together with his rusticity and his quiet ways, were in themselves enough to make Jackson a class oddity. But there was more. He had begun to develop eccentricities related to his health, doing curious things in the name of physical fitness. He would pump an arm up and down for some minutes, keeping a careful count and fretting if someone interrupted him. When sitting, he usually kept himself rigidly erect, not only because this seemed to facilitate his digestion but because he believed that compressing one's intestines made them subject to disease.

At first the wisecrackers and practical jokers of the class concentrated on Jackson, expecting him to provide them high sport. But his natural shrewdness, sharpened by the diverse responsibilities of his previous years, enabled him to thwart most of their best efforts. And even when they managed to put him at a disadvantage, he showed so little concern that they gained no satisfaction. They soon gave up the game.

Jackson obeyed the academy's rules to the best of his ability, adjusting well to the rigid discipline. But he ignored the social traditions. He had few intimates, impressing his classmates as being largely self-contained; his home ties, maintained by letter, seemed enough to sustain him. It was clear that he regarded the academy as first of all a center of instruction.

A glimpse of Cadet Jackson's struggles during the first winter is given by P. T. Turnley, the classmate already quoted:

We were studying algebra and analytical geometry . . . and Jackson was very low in his class. Just before the signal "lights out" he would pile up his grate with anthracite coal, and lying prone before it on the floor would work away at his lessons by the glare of the fire, which scorched his very brain, till a late hour of the night. . . .

If he could not master the portion of the textbook assigned for the day he would not pass over it but continued to work at it till he understood it. Thus [in the classroom] it often happened that when he was called out to repeat his task he had to reply that he had not yet reached the lesson of the day but was employed upon the previous one. There was no alternative but to mark him as unprepared, a proceeding which did not in the least affect his resolution.

Says another classmate:

No one I have ever known could so perfectly withdraw his mind from surrounding objects or influences, and so thoroughly involve his whole being in the subject under consideration. His lessons were uppermost in his mind, and to thoroughly understand them was always his determined effort. To make the author's knowledge his own was ever the point at which he aimed.

This intense application of mind was naturally strengthened by constant exercise, and month by month, and year by year, his faculties of perception developed rapidly, until he grasped with unerring quickness the inceptive points of all ethical and mathematical problems.

As Jackson's mind grew keener, so did his devotion to duty, his self-dependence, and his ambition. Foremost among a set of maxims he compiled during this period was "You can be what you resolve to be."

The growth of his ambition in no way compromised Jackson's honesty. It was, indeed, so great that he could not tolerate dishonesty in others. When a cadet switched a dirty musket for Jackson's clean one and presented it as his own at inspection, Jackson not only exposed him through a secret mark on the weapon but urged the officers that he be court-martialed. Only by the most strenuous persuasion on the part of the officers and his comrades could Jackson be induced to waive his right to press the charge.

But Jackson could be equally earnest in his support for a cadet in honest trouble. And, in spite of the limits he placed on his social contacts, he kept a sympathetic ear ready for any comrade who needed it. Moreover, those who fell sick could always count on him for tender attention.

Again in the words of P. T. Turnley:

I believe he went through the very trying ordeal of the four years at West Point without ever having a hard word or a bad feeling from cadet or professor. While there were many who seemed to surpass him in intellect, in geniality, and in good fellowship, there was no one of our class who more absolutely possessed the respect and confidence of all; and in the end "Old Jack," as he was always called, with his desperate earnestness, his unflinching straightforwardness, and his high sense of honor, came to be regarded by his comrades with something very like affection.

The class graduated on July 1, 1846. Cadet Jackson had worked his way up from fifty-first to seventeenth—a considerable accomplishment. Those who knew him best claimed that if the training had lasted another year he would have been first. The class, incidentally, included George B. McClellan, George E. Pickett, Ambrose P. Hill, and others destined to make names for themselves in the Civil War.

Jackson, now twenty-two years old (and calling himself Thomas Jonathan Jackson, having taken his father's name as his middle name), became a brevet second lieutenant of artillery—a brevet being a nomi-

nal rank rather than an official one. The Mexican War had begun, and about six weeks after his graduation, Jackson was ordered to the war zone, being assigned to Company K, First Regiment of United States Artillery.

He saw no action during the first six months and was worried that the war might end before his regiment was sent to the front. More than once he was heard to exclaim, "How I should like to be in one battle!"

On March 3, 1847, Jackson's rank as second lieutenant was made official. Six days later he took part in the landing near Vera Cruz, on Mexico's Gulf Coast, with a thirteen-thousand-man force under General Winfield Scott. Bombarded by land and sea, Vera Cruz fell on March 27. Jackson was credited with "gallant and meritorious conduct" under fire, which gained him the brevet of first lieutenant.

General Scott soon launched his invading army on a march of about 250 miles toward Mexico City. Along the way were fought the battles of Cerro Gordo, Contreras, Cherubusco, and Molino del Rey. Jackson did his best work at Contreras. According to his commanding officer, Captain John Bankhead Magruder:

... Lieutenant Jackson, commanding the second section of the battery ... advanced in handsome style, and ... kept up the fire [already begun by the battery's first section] with great briskness and effect. His conduct was equally conspicuous during the whole day. ...

At length Scott's army drew up before Chapultepec, a castle-fortress that guarded the road to Mexico City, the city being three miles farther on. Chapultepec was assaulted on September 13, with Jackson seeing heavy action. One of the other young officers present was Daniel H. Hill, who relates:

Lieutenant Jackson's section of Magruder's battery was subjected to a plunging fire from the Castle of Chapultepec. The little six-pounders could effect nothing against the guns of the Mexicans, of much heavier calibre, firing from an elevation. The horses were killed or disabled, and the men [who were also suffering from the fire] became so demoralized that they deserted the guns and sought shelter behind a wall or embankment. Lieutenant Jackson remained at the guns, walking back and forth, and kept saying, "See, there is no danger; I am not hit!"

WINFIELD SCOTT.

Jackson said in afteryears that his statement about the lack of danger was the only wilful falsehood he ever told in his life.

For a time Jackson fired one of the guns himself, aided by a single brave sergeant. The peril subsided when the infantry attack, which had been bloodied and temporarily stalled, went forward again. Jackson went forward, too, and soon his guns were helping to sweep the enemy from the streets about the castle. His success, however, was marred by a moment of profound regret; some demoralized civilians got in the way of one of his discharges.

Daniel Hill continues:

When the castle was captured, many of the stormers dispersed in search of plunder and liquor. A few [infantry troops] pursued promptly the retreating column of Mexicans . . . towards the Garita of San Cosme [one of the gates of Mexico City].... After the chase had been continued over a mile, Lieutenant Jackson came up with two pieces of artillery.... Captain Magruder himself soon appeared with caissons [ammunition wagons] and men.... Shortly after the arrival of Captain Magruder, a column of two thousand [enemy] cavalry... made a demonstration of charging upon the guns. They were unlimbered, and a rapid fire was opened upon the Mexicans, who retreated without attacking....

When the American infantry came up in force, the advance was continued to the city's gate, where it was stopped for a time by fresh troops. Before the day was done, the attackers had gained a hold inside the city's walls. The city surrendered on September 14, and this virtually ended the war.

Jackson's heroism in front of Chapultepec, capping his earlier work, prompted Captain Magruder to say in his report:

If devotion, industry, talent, and gallantry are the highest qualities of a soldier, then he is entitled to the distinction which their possession confers. I have been ably seconded in all the operations of the battery by him; and upon this occasion [at Chapultepec], when circumstances placed him in command, for a short time, of an independent section, he proved himself eminently worthy of it.

For gallantry at Contreras, Jackson had been brevetted a captain; his work at Chapultepec won him the brevet of major. None of his West Point comrades made so great a stride in rank.

Asked whether he had been afraid for his life while achieving this record, Jackson replied: "No, the only anxiety of which I was conscious during the engagements was a fear lest I should not meet danger enough to make my conduct conspicuous."

Also distinguishing themselves in Scott's campaign were a number of others who, like Jackson, were later to become famous. Among them were Ulysses S. Grant and Robert E. Lee.

Shortly after the Americans established their occupation of Mexico City, General Scott held a reception for his officers, some of the younger of whom he had never met. He had heard of Jackson's accomplishments, but when Jackson was presented to him, he did not extend his hand at once but pretended to be displeased, saying with a frown: "If you can

JACKSON at the
close of the
Mexican War.

*forgive yourself for the way you slaughtered those poor Mexicans with
your guns, I am not sure that I can!"*

*Having thus caught the attention of all in the room, and having set
Jackson blushing in confusion, Scott broke into a smile and thrust out
his hand. The joke was not in the best of taste, but one of the men who
heard it said later: "No greater compliment could have been paid a
young officer."*

*Jackson's textbook knowledge of war had now been augmented by
hard practical experience. He had learned not only some valuable
strategic and tactical lessons but also the ways of human nature under
fire and how men must be handled. He had learned, too, that his own
courage was unshakable and that battle sharpened his judgment. These
things added essentially to his stature and self-confidence as an officer.*

During the protracted negotiations that gained the vast territories of California and New Mexico for the United States, Scott's army remained in possession of the Mexican capital. The citizens, learning that the Americans were disposed to be friendly and had money to spend, became the warmest of hosts.

Jackson, having few duties to perform, joined his comrades in enjoying the city's social life. Since dancing was a prominent part of this life—and offered a fine opportunity for getting to know the women—Jackson took it up, though the movements must have taxed his sluggish reflexes to the utmost.

He found the brunette senoritas fascinating, and he studied the Spanish language so as to be able to converse with them. He was drawn to one girl in particular, but through his uncommon self-control he managed to keep the relationship from going farther than he considered wise.

Jackson's knowledge of the language became proficient enough for him to read a number of books in Spanish, among them a history of Mexico. And aided by Mexican priests and the Archbishop of Mexico himself, he made an extensive study of the Roman Catholic religion, for he felt that it was soon time he embraced a definite creed. But he did not commit himself to Catholicism.

The occupation of the city ended in June 1848. Along with the rest of the army, Jackson and his battery returned to the port of Vera Cruz and embarked for the United States.

⤳ II.

The Virginia
Military Institute

⤳ *Assigned to Fort Hamilton, on Long Island, near the entrance
of New York harbor, the young major began a life dominated by routine
peacetime duties. Much of his spare time was spent in reading to expand
his knowledge, with emphasis being placed on history, both military and
political.*

*He consulted New York City's best physicians about his stomach trou-
ble and other chronic discomforts, but got little relief. This prompted him
to increase his reliance on self-treatment, largely in the areas of diet and
exercise. Some of Jackson's complaints were very strange ones. He
doubtless had some real health problems, but he apparently had a strong
streak of hypochondria as well. Says his old West Point classmate,
Dabney Maury, who had become an instructor at the Point and was one
day surprised by a visit from Jackson:*

At that time he was convinced that one of his legs was bigger
than the other, and that one of his arms was likewise unduly
heavy. He had acquired the habit of raising the heavy arm
straight up so that, as he said, the blood would run back into his
body and lighten it. I believe he never after relinquished this
peculiar practice. . . .

*While at Fort Hamilton, Jackson looked deeper into the Christian reli-
gion, with his apprehensions about his health adding to his already
strong interest. He began to believe that his afflictions had been decreed*

12

by God to punish him for his sins and to put him on the road to salvation. Not certain that he had been baptized as a child, he had this ceremony performed.

Granted a furlough in December 1848, the major visited his relatives in western Virginia. It wasn't a happy trip; a favorite uncle had just died, and an aunt was found on her deathbed. (Jackson's brother, incidentally, had died seven years earlier, having reached but the age of twenty. His sister, however, now Mrs. Jonathan Arnold, was destined for a long life.)

Late in the year 1850 Jackson was transferred from New York to Fort Meade, Florida. Somewhat restless in a peacetime army, he was soon at odds with his new commanding officer, whom he felt was not giving him enough responsibility. A different kind of trouble developed when it was rumored that the commander was having an affair with his children's nursemaid and Jackson considered it his duty to undertake an investigation! The resulting scandal not only rocked the post but reached the public. The commander was transferred.

Jackson himself soon left the post—and the army—for a civil pursuit. He was selected to fill an opening at the Virginia Military Institute, located at Lexington, at the southern end of the Shenandoah Valley. Resigning his commission, he reported to Lexington in the early autumn of 1851. Among the officials at the Institute at the time was William B. Taliaferro, who writes:

... as one of the members of the Visitorial Board ... I found him the newly appointed professor of natural philosophy and instructor of artillery.... The impression he produced upon me ... was that he was a man of peculiarities, quite distinctly marked from other people—reserved, yet polite; reticent of opinions but fixed in the ideas he had formed; essentially averse to obtruding them upon others, but determined and un-flinching in their advocacy when pressed to any expression of them.

Adds James H. Lane, who became a cadet at the Institute as Jackson's career began:

That quiet ... and dignified new professor ... soon impressed that corps of high-toned but mischievous young Virginians as being a man of intense individuality of character. He was conscientious ... in the discharge of every duty and strictly just in all his intentions.

One of the youths who reported to the Institute at the start of Jackson's
second year was a distant relative he had never met, sixteen-year-old
John G. Gittings. Jackson surprised Gittings by sending for him.

On receiving this order [Gittings relates], my first thought
was that I had violated . . . one of the innumerable military rules
and was about to be called to an account therefor; so it was with
some trepidation that I went to the major's quarters. However,
he met me with a smile and greeting that somewhat relieved my
anxiety, but . . . I still felt some awe in the presence of this
military officer in full uniform, whom I had been told was a
stern and rigid disciplinarian.

The major took my cap, placed it carefully on the table, then
made me take the best chair in the room, after which he took a
seat himself and, with apparently a labored effort, tried to
make things pleasant. Though entertaining, he appeared ill at
ease; and this, I noticed afterward, was characteristic of him
when conversing in the presence of strangers. . . .

He was then about twenty-eight years of age, six feet tall, with
gray-blue eyes, a well-chiseled Roman nose, and a very fair and
ruddy countenance. He wore side-whiskers, and one noting his
very fair complexion and reserved manner might have mistaken
him for an Englishman, but here the resemblance ceased, for in
thought and expression this quiet, unaffected man was all
American. As I sat in his presence and observed his diffidence,
this thought passed through my mind: Can this modest man be
the one who fought so bravely in Mexico and who stood by his
cannon after all his men had been killed or driven away?

. . . At the artillery practice . . . Major Jackson was a very strict
and exacting officer. He expected every man to do his duty. . . .
One day . . . a fellow plebe [one of a prankish nature] managed
in some way to draw out a linchpin from a wheel of the limber
at which I was pulling [with a team of horses], and, as a conse-
quence, in trotting down an incline at a fast pace, the wheel flew
off with considerable force, and, as the fates would have it,
rolled directly toward "Old Jack," who was looking in an opposite direction.

He turned his head in time to see its approach, and although
it passed within a few inches of his person, he did not budge
from his tracks. A cadet remarked: "He would not have moved
if it had been a cannonball going right through him!"

But we soon observed that his gaze was fixed intently on our battery in a way that made us feel very uncomfortable, and in a brief space we were placed under arrest—officers, cannoneers, horses, and all; and . . . this breach of discipline was settled in a way that did not invite any repetition of the offence.

Though Jackson was able enough as an artillery instructor, he was not a good classroom teacher. Having no background in his subjects (optics, analytical mechanics, acoustics, and astronomy), he was obliged to study as he taught, keeping only a step ahead of his students. Bored by his lectures, some of the youths resorted to pranks against him—this in spite of the certainty of stern punishment if they were caught.

At least one student, writing home, called Jackson "such a hell of a fool" when it came to teaching. Another, having received a bad mark he blamed on the professor, put him down as "crazy as damnation."

Jackson eventually improved his techniques, though he was never called more than "a conscientious, laborious instructor."

Reflecting on Jackson's general dealings with his students and with other people, John Gittings calls him "one of the most scrupulously truthful men that ever lived."

He . . . even carried his exactitude of expression and performance to extremes in small matters. On one occasion he borrowed the key of a library of one of the literary societies, and promised the secretary to return it within an hour. However, becoming absorbed in his book, he put the key into his pocket and did not think of it again until he had reached his boarding place in the town, nearly a mile away.

Then, although a hard storm had sprung up in the meantime, he turned about and marched all the way back through the rain to deliver the key as he had promised, though he knew the library would not be used and the key would not be needed on that day.

In conversation, if he ever happened to make an ironical remark, even if it were so plainly ironical that none could misapprehend it, yet would he invariably qualify his expression by saying, "Not meaning exactly what I say." This peculiarity of speech became almost a byword with the cadets and subjected him to much embarrassment, but such was his regard for truth that he would not depart from it, even in jest, without immediately correcting his statement.

An unnamed woman who knew Jackson well at this time interjects:

When it would be playfully represented to him that this needless precision interfered with the graces of conversation, and tended to give angularity and stiffness to his style, his reply would be that he was perfectly aware of the inelegance it involved, but he chose to sacrifice all minor charms to the paramount one of absolute truth.

Now in his latter twenties, Jackson decided it was time he married, and he began seeking a bride among the area's more devout Christian families.

Jackson himself, after his years of indecision, had settled upon Presbyterianism, the denomination of his ancestors. He was an official in the local church, and he viewed the Sabbath with infinite reverence. He refused to travel on that day, and he tried to regulate the letters he mailed so they reached their destinations without doing so. He even felt that Sundays should be kept free of worldly conversation, and he would sometimes say to an offender, "Let us talk about that tomorrow."

But, strange to say, Jackson's observance of the Sabbath was often flawed. While sitting through long sermons, he had a way of falling asleep, his chin on his chest. The cadets who saw him were highly amused, though Gittings says they attributed these lapses not to boredom but to "physical weakness."

Gittings continues:

Speaking from a social standpoint, no man ever had a more delicate regard for the feelings of others than he . . . and while his manner was often constrained, and even awkward, yet he would usually make a favorable impression through his evident desire to please. However . . . he was generally underrated by his casual acquaintances, for in such society he was a taciturn man and would listen in silence while others discoursed at length upon subjects in which he himself was well versed. He would thus create a false impression of his own acquirements, which were very considerable . . . and embraced a wide knowledge of men and things.

About the second year of my stay at the Virginia Military Institute, Major Jackson was suffering from weak eyes, and he would not read by artificial light. . . . When, near one of the examinations, our class . . . prevailed on him to give us a review of a difficult study, he was compelled to hear us after dark, the only time he had to spare for the purpose. We used to meet in the "section room" in the dark. Professor Jackson sat in front of us on his platform and, with closed eyes, questioned us over . . . a complicated study. This work required a strong effort of memory and concentration of thought.

Jackson married Eleanor Junkin, daughter of the Rev. Dr. George Junkin, president of Washington College, another Lexington institution, in 1853. The union, Gittings explains, was a short one:

Major Jackson had the great misfortune to lose his wife the second year of his marriage. [She died delivering a lifeless child.] The Rev. Dr. [William S.] White, an aged minister of the Presbyterian church, officiated at the funeral, to which the cadets marched as a guard of honor.

After the services were over at the grave and the attendants had all left the grounds except the cadets, who were forming their ranks [to do the same] . . . it was noticed that Jackson was standing alone, with uncovered head, by the open grave, as one distraught. The venerable minister, who was a lame man, was compelled to hobble all the way back from the gate and lead him away, as he would heed none other.

This funeral took place in the autumn of 1854. For a long time the thirty-year-old Jackson paid daily visits to the grave. In mid-winter he wrote to an aunt: "I can hardly realize yet that my dear Ellie is no more—that she will never again welcome my return, no more soothe my troubled spirit by her ever kind, sympathizing heart, words, and love." In a notebook, he wrote: "Objects to be effected by Ellie's death: To eradicate ambition; to eradicate resentment; to produce humility." Slowly the wound began to heal.

In 1856, Jackson spent his summer vacation in Europe, traveling widely in the British Isles, Belgium, France, Germany, Switzerland, and Italy. He found himself enjoying "an almost inexhaustible assemblage of grand and beautiful associations," and was particularly impressed with Italy's painting and sculpture. He was drawn to the French language, and picked up enough of it to enable him to read in a French Bible.

His return steamer was delayed in its passage of the Atlantic, and he was late for the start of the fall term at the Institute. His friends, knowing him to be the very soul of punctuality, asked whether he had not been beside himself with impatience and worry when he knew he was going to be late. He replied, "Not at all. I did all in my power to be here at the appointed time. When the steamer was delayed by Providence, my responsibility was at an end."

Since it was now two years since his wife died, Jackson had begun thinking in terms of taking another. Even before he married Eleanor Junkin, he had met another young woman who appealed to him: Miss Mary Anna Morrison, of North Carolina. Like Eleanor, she was the daughter of a clergyman. During the summer of Jackson's engagement to Eleanor, Mary Anna and her sister Eugenia had visited in Lexington, and Jackson had served as their escort on a number of occasions.

Mary Anna takes up the narrative:

We had heard with sincere sorrow and sympathy of the death of Mrs. Jackson; but afterwards nothing was heard from the major. . . . However . . . after returning from Europe with restored health and spirits he began to realize that life could be made bright and happy to him again, and . . . his first impulse was to open communication with his old friend . . . and see if she could not be induced to become a participant in attaining his desired happiness. So, to my great surprise, the first letter I ever received from him came to me expressing such blissful memories . . . of the summer we had been together in Lexington that my sister Eugenia laughed most heartily over it and predicted an early visit from the major.

Still, I was incredulous, and when her prediction was verified in a very short time and I saw a tall form in military dress walking up from my father's gate I could scarcely believe my senses. . . . My father was highly pleased with him as a Christian gentleman, and my mother was also favorably impressed, especially with his extreme politeness, so that his visit was one of mutual congeniality and enjoyment. . . .

On the 16th of July, 1857, we were married. It was a quiet little home wedding. . . . His bridal gifts to me were a beautiful gold watch and a lovely set of seed pearls. A few days after our marriage we set out upon a Northern tour. The trip included visits to Richmond, Baltimore, Philadelphia, New York, Saratoga, and Niagara. In New York we saw almost everything that was to be seen in the way of sight-seeing, even climbing to the top of the spire of Trinity Church. . . . The view was grand indeed. . . . But the places that combined the greatest amount of interest and pleasure were Niagara and Saratoga. . . . At Saratoga he took not a particle of interest in the gay and fashionable throng, but the natural beauties of the place charmed him, and he found a delightful recreation in rowing me over the lovely lake, whose placid waters were, at that time, covered with water-lilies.

After completing this delightful Northern tour, we wended our way to the Rockbridge Alum Springs, a very pleasant mountain resort in the Valley of Virginia, and only a few hours from Lexington. Here we remained several weeks . . . spending the time in reading, walking, and sitting in the woods. . . . Major Jackson derived great benefit from the mineral waters of the Rockbridge Alum Springs, and it was a favorite resort of his.

Upon our return to Lexington we lived . . . at the best hotel in the place; but he was not at all fond of boarding, and longed for . . . a home of his own. . . . After boarding more than a year, he finally succeeded in purchasing a house in Lexington, the only available one he could obtain. . . . He lost no time in going to work to repair it and make it comfortable and attractive. His tastes were simple, but he liked to have everything in perfect order—every door "on golden hinges softly turning," as he expressed it . . . and under his methodical management his household soon became as regular and well-ordered as it was possible for it to be with Negro servants. . . .

He was intensely fond of his home, and it was there he found his greatest happiness. There all that was best in his nature shone forth. . . . He was generous but unostentatious in his mode of living, and nothing gave him more pleasure than to welcome his friends [few in number but very firm] to his simple and hospitable home. He particularly delighted in entertaining ministers of the Gospel.

His garden was a source of very great pleasure to him: he worked in it a great deal with his own hands, and cultivated it in quite a scientific way. He . . . raised more vegetables than his family could consume. His early training upon his uncle's farm had instilled into him a love for rural pursuits, and it was not long until he gratified his desire to possess a little farm of his own, which embraced twenty acres near town. Here, with the aid of his Negroes, he raised wheat, corn, and other products. . . .

His life at home was perfectly regular and systematic. He arose about six o'clock, and first knelt in secret prayer. Then he took a cold bath, which was never omitted even in the coldest days of winter. This was followed by a brisk walk, in rain or shine . . . and he returned looking the picture of freshness and animation.

During these walks, Jackson would sometimes stop abruptly and raise his "heavy" arm to drain some of its blood, a practice that made Lexington's citizens shake their heads. Mary Anna continues:

Seven o'clock was the hour for family prayers, which he required all his servants to attend promptly and regularly. He never waited for anyone, not even his wife. Breakfast followed prayers, after which he left immediately for the Institute, his classes opening at eight o'clock and continuing until eleven. He was engaged in teaching only three hours a day, except for a few weeks before the close of the session, when the artillery practice demanded an additional hour in the afternoon.

Upon his return home at eleven o'clock, he devoted himself to study until one. The first book he took up . . . was his Bible, which he read with a commentary, and the many pencil marks upon it showed with what care he bent over its pages. From his Bible lesson he turned to his textbooks, which engaged him until dinner, at one o'clock. During these hours of study he would not permit any interruption, and stood all that time in front of a high desk, which he had made to order. . . .

After dinner he gave himself up for half an hour or more to leisure and conversation, and this was one of the brightest periods in the home life. He then went into his garden, or out to his farm to superintend his servants, and frequently joined them in manual labor. He would often drive me out to the farm and find a shady spot for me under the trees while he attended to the work of the field. When this was not the case, he always returned in time to take me, if the weather permitted, for an evening walk or drive. In summer we often took our drives by moonlight. . . .

When at home he would indulge himself in a season of rest and recreation after supper, thinking it was injurious to health to go to work immediately. As it was a rule with him never to use his eyes by artificial light, he formed the habit of studying mentally for an hour or so without a book. After going over his lessons in the morning, he thus reviewed them at night; and in order to abstract his thoughts from surrounding objects—a habit which he had cultivated to a remarkable degree—he would, if alone with his wife, ask that he might not be disturbed by any conversation, and he would then take his seat with his face to the wall and remain in perfect abstraction until he finished his mental task, when he would emerge with a bright and cheerful face into social enjoyment again. He was very fond of being read to, and much of our time in the evenings was passed in my ministering to him in this way. . . .

He had a library which, though small, was select, composed chiefly of scientific, historical, and religious books [but giving an honored place to Shakespeare], with some of a lighter character, and some in Spanish and French. Nearly all of them were full of his pencil marks, made with a view to future reference.

The few years spent so happily and peacefully in this little home were unmarked by any events important to the outside world. One little bud of promise was sent for a brief period to awaken new hopes of domestic joy and comfort. . . . The father, in announcing the arrival of the infant to its [maternal] grandmother [by mail], commences thus: "Dear Mother—we have in our home circle a darling little namesake of yours. . . ." And he concluded by saying: "I hope it will not be many years before our little Mary Graham will be able to send sweet little messages to you all."

The child lived only a few weeks, and its loss was a great, very great, sorrow to him. But here, as always, religion subdued every murmur. Great as was his love for children, his spirit of submission was greater, and even in this bitter disappointment he bowed uncomplainingly to his Father's will.

The summer of 1858 . . . was spent at the North. . . . He was fond of traveling and liked the bracing climate of the Northern States. . . . He always returned home much refreshed and benefited by these excursions.... The opening of the fall term of the Military Institute always found him at his post, and our return home was a joyful time both to us and our domestics. . . .

He was a very strict but kind master, giving to his servants "that which is just and equal," but exacting of them prompt obedience.... His... system soon showed its good effects. They realized that if they did their duty they would receive the best of treatment from him. At Christmas he was generous in presents, and [through the year] frequently gave them small sums of money.

There was one . . . little servant in the family, named Emma, whom the master took under his sheltering roof at the solicitation of an aged lady in town, to whom the child became a care after having been left an orphan. . . . She was not bright, but he persevered in drilling her into memorizing a child's catechism, and it was a most amusing picture to see her standing before him with fixed attention, as if she were straining every nerve, and reciting her answers with the drop of a curtsy at each word. She had not been taught to do this, but it was such an effort for her to learn that she assumed this motion involuntarily. . . .

A little incident will show the kindness and tenderness of his heart. A gentleman who spent the night with us was accompanied by his daughter, but four years of age. It was the first time the child had been separated from her mother. . . . After the guests had both sunk into slumber, the father was aroused by someone leaning over his little girl and drawing the covering more closely around her. It was only his thoughtful host, who felt anxious lest his little guest should miss her mother's guardian care under his roof, and he could not go to sleep himself until he was satisfied that all was well with the child.

In his home no man could have been more unrestrained and demonstrative, and his buoyancy and sportiveness were quite a revelation to me when I became a sharer in the privacy of his inmost life. . . .

One morning he returned from a very early artillery drill, for which he had donned full regimentals . . . and he never looked more noble and handsome than when he entered his chamber [i.e., the couple's bedroom], sword in hand. He playfully began to brandish the sword over his wife's head, looking as ferocious and terrible as a veritable Bluebeard, and asking her if she was not afraid.

His acting was so realistic that for a moment the timid little woman did quail, which he no sooner saw than he threw down his sword, and, in a perfect outburst of glee, speedily transformed himself into the very antipode of a wife-killer.

He would often hide himself behind a door at the sound of the approaching footstep of his wife, and spring out to greet her with a startling caress.

During the spring of 1859 I was not well, and as he always wished me to have the best medical attention the country afforded, he took me to New York for treatment, where I was obliged to remain several weeks. As it was the time of his session, he could not stay with me, so he had to return to his duties and spend all those weeks by himself. It was our first separation.... Every day that a letter could make the trip *without travelling on Sunday* he was heard from....

It was in the fall of 1859 that the celebrated John Brown raid was made upon the government stores at Harpers Ferry [in that part of Virginia soon to become West Virginia]. Brown was a fanatic who conceived the idea that he could raise an insurrection in the South and emancipate the Negroes. But he was arrested, convicted, and condemned to execution.

Fearing that an attempt might be made to rescue him, the Governor of Virginia . . . ordered out the troops, in which were included the corps of cadets of the Virginia Military Institute; and with their officers at their head they marched to the place of rendezvous [i.e., to Charles Town, near Harpers Ferry, where the execution was to take place]. The following extracts from Major Jackson's letters will tell the part he had to take in the affair:

"Charles Town, Nov. 28, 1859. I reached here last night in good health and spirits.... There are about one thousand troops here, and everything is quiet so far. We don't expect any trouble. The excitement is confined to more distant points."

"December 2d. John Brown was hung today at about half past eleven A.M. He behaved with unflinching firmness.... The gibbet was erected in a large field, southeast of the town. Brown

JOHN BROWN.

rode on the head of his coffin from his prison to the place of execution.... The jailer, high-sheriff, and several others rode in the same wagon with the prisoner. Brown ... ascended the scaffold with apparent cheerfulness.

"After reaching the top ... he shook hands with several who were standing around him. The sheriff placed the rope around his neck, then threw a white cap over his head and asked him if he wished a signal when all should be ready. He replied that it made no difference, provided he was not kept waiting too long.

"In this condition he stood for about ten minutes on the trapdoor ... when the rope was cut by a single blow, and Brown fell through.... With the fall, his arms, below the elbows, flew up horizontally, his hands clinched.... His arms gradually fell ... by spasmodic motions. There was very little motion of his person for several moments, and soon the wind blew his lifeless body to and fro....

"[Before the drop] I was much impressed with the thought that before me stood a man in the full vigor of health, who must in a few moments enter eternity. I sent up the petition that he might be saved [from hell].... He refused to have a minister with him.... His body was taken back to the jail, and at six o'clock P.M. was sent to his wife at Harpers Ferry....

"We leave for home via Richmond tomorrow."

On his return to Lexington, Jackson resumed his duties at the Institute. The town at this time held a newcomer, young Henry Kyd Douglas, who was attending a private law school. He met Jackson, and his interest was sparked:

I ... said to a classmate in the law school, who had been at the Institute: "It seems to me ... I'd like to know Major Jackson better. There is something about him I can't make out."

"Nobody can. But it wouldn't pay.... Old Jack's a character, genius, or just a little crazy, or something of that sort. He lives quietly and don't meddle with people; but he is as systematic as a multiplication table, and as full of military as an arsenal. Stiff, you see ... but kindhearted as a woman.... But mind what I say—if this John Brown business leads to war, he'll be heard from."

At this time, says Mary Anna Jackson,

... Major Jackson was strongly for the Union, but at the same time he was a firm States'-rights man.... He was never a secessionist, and maintained that it was better for the South to fight for her rights *in the Union than out of it.*

The grand old State of Virginia ... was among the last of the Southern States to secede. South Carolina, after her secession ... bombarded Fort Sumter [a Federal installation in Charleston Harbor], which in a short time was reduced.... President Lincoln then issued a proclamation, calling upon the States to furnish seventy-five thousand men to put down what he assumed to be a rebellion.... Virginia now hesitated no longer. On the 17th of April [1861] she seceded, and immediately began preparations for the struggle which was inevitable.

After the threat of coercion on the part of the North, the South became almost a unit, and the enthusiasm with which men of all ages and classes rushed to arms was only equalled by that of the women at home....

Mary Anna goes on to explain that it was later to be said of Jackson that he went to war "for slavery and the Southern Confederacy, with the unshaken conviction that both were to endure."

... I am very confident that he would never have fought for the sole object of perpetuating slavery. It was for her *constitutional rights* that the South resisted the North, and slavery was only comprehended among those rights.

He found the institution [of slavery] a responsible and troublesome one, and I have heard him say that he would prefer to see the Negroes free, but he believed that the Bible taught that slavery was sanctioned by the Creator himself, who maketh men to differ and instituted laws for the bond and the free. He therefore accepted slavery, as it existed in the Southern States, not as a thing desirable in itself but as allowed by Providence for ends which it was not his business to determine. . . .

At the time that the clouds of war were about to burst over the land, the Presbytery of Lexington held its spring meeting in the church which Major Jackson attended. . . . Jackson was entertaining some of the members of this body, but owing to the intense political excitement in the town and the constant demands made upon him in military matters, he found but little time to give to his guests. . . .

The cadets were wild with youthful ardor at the prospect of war, and the citizens were forming volunteer companies, drilling and equipping to enter the service. Major Jackson's practical wisdom and energy were much sought after, and inspired hope and confidence. . . .

The Governor of the State . . . notified the superintendent of the Institute that he should need the services of the more advanced classes of the cadets as drill-masters, and they must be prepared to go to Richmond at a moment's notice, under the command of Major Jackson.

Having been almost entirely absorbed all the week with his military occupations, to the exclusion of his attendance upon a single church service . . . he expressed the earnest hope, on retiring late Saturday night, that the call to Richmond would not come before Monday, and that he might be permitted to spend a quiet Sabbath. . . .

But Heaven ordered it otherwise. About the dawn of that

Sabbath morning, April 21st, our doorbell rang, and the order came that Major Jackson should bring the cadets to Richmond immediately.... Without waiting for breakfast, he repaired at once to the Institute.... Finding that several hours of preparation would necessarily be required, he appointed the hour for starting at one o'clock P.M. He sent a message to his pastor, Dr. White, requesting him to come to the barracks and offer a prayer with the command before its departure.

All the morning he was engaged at the Institute, allowing himself only a short time to return to his home about eleven o'clock, when he took a hurried breakfast and completed a few necessary preparations for his journey.

Then, in the privacy of our chamber, he took his Bible and read that beautiful chapter in Corinthians beginning with the sublime hope of the resurrection . . . and then, kneeling down, he committed himself and her whom he loved to the protecting care of his Father in heaven.... His voice was so choked with emotion that he could scarcely utter the words, and one of his most earnest petitions was that "if consistent with His will, God would still avert the threatening danger and grant us peace!"

... When Dr. White went to the Institute to hold the short religious service which Major Jackson requested, the latter told him the command would march precisely at one o'clock, and the minister, knowing his punctuality, made it a point to close the service at a quarter before one.

... after waiting a few moments, an officer approached Major Jackson and said: "Major, everything is now ready. May we not set out?" The only reply he made was to point to the dial-plate of the barracks clock, and not until the hand pointed to the hour of one was his voice heard to ring out the order, "Forward, march!"

From this time forth the life of my husband belonged to his beloved Southern land, and his private life becomes public history.

~III.

Harpers Ferry and
Falling Waters

⌇Major Jackson and his cadets made the greater part of their journey by rail, and by nightfall of the second day, April 22, 1861, they were establishing themselves in a training camp that was mushrooming on the Richmond fairgrounds, about a mile and a half from the city.

The troops converging there, all possessed by the war fever, included not only Virginians but residents of other Southern states. From all walks of life, both urban and rural, they ranged from smooth-faced boys to men with white beards. Some wore militia uniforms; others were decked in colorful costumes of their own styling; and still others appeared in ordinary civilian clothes. They carried an assortment of muskets, shotguns, pistols, and swords; and some of the units marched with red-coated Negro fifers and drummers in front.

Great crowds of civilians assembled to watch, encourage, and aid the proceedings, with the ladies contributing their sewing and cooking skills and also their smiles and flirtatious glances.

On April 23, John B. Jones, a clerk in the Richmond war offices, wrote in his diary:

The cadets of the Military Institute are rendering good service [as drill instructors] now, and Professor Jackson is truly a benefactor. I hope he will take the field [as a combat officer] ... and if he does, I predict for him a successful career.

Jackson himself anticipated a quick assignment to the field, and when his wife wrote him for permission to join him at Richmond, he answered:

"I would like very much to see my sweet little face, but my darling had better remain at her own home, as my continuance here is very uncertain."

On April 27 the governor of Virginia, John Letcher, commissioned Jackson a colonel of volunteers and ordered him to take command at Harpers Ferry. The move was endorsed by General Robert E. Lee, recently placed in charge of all of Virginia's armed forces.

Harpers Ferry, at the junction of the Shenandoah and Potomac rivers and of importance as the northern gateway to the Shenandoah Valley, had been seized by Confederate troops nine days earlier. The Federals of the arsenal had been obliged to abandon the installation, though they destroyed much of it as they left.

Colonel Jackson reached Harpers Ferry about May 1. Says Mary Anna Jackson:

The first news from him . . . was simply a line of Spanish, expressing all the love of his heart. The second was not much longer, but in it he said: "I am very much gratified with my command. . . . I am in tolerable health, probably a little better than usual, if I had enough sleep. I haven't time now to do more than to tell you how much I love you."

. . . In [another] letter he advised me to make every necessary provision for the servants and arrange all our home interests so that I could return to my father's sheltering roof in North Carolina. . . .

Our servants . . . had up to this time remained at home; but without the firm guidance and restraint of their master, the excitement of the times proved so demoralizing to them that he deemed it best for me to provide them with good homes among the permanent residents.

After doing this, packing our furniture, and closing our house, my burdened, anxious heart found sweet relief and comfort upon reaching the home of my kind parents, who had sent one of my young brothers to bring me to them. . . . Thenceforward my home was with them throughout the war, except during the few visits which I was permitted to pay my husband in the army.

Before Jackson's arrival, the troops occupying Harpers Ferry, several thousand in number, had been commanded by a set of gaudily uniformed militia generals who placed more emphasis on pomp and ceremony than on practical matters. Since most of the state's militia officers

ROBERT E. LEE.

were of this mold, being little more than civilians in uniform, the gov-
ernment at Richmond had issued an ordinance deposing all militia
officers above the rank of captain, the object being to tighten and
strengthen the state's command system. Thus Colonel Jackson and his
two aides, a colonel and a major, found themselves replacing several
generals and a large staff.

The troops themselves were undisciplined, considering themselves to
be on something of a lark. An enlisted man, John N. Opie, tells of one of
Jackson's first acts:

Finding that there were great quantities of liquor in the town,
he ordered it to be poured out. The barrels were brought forth,
the heads knocked in, and the contents poured into the gutter.
But the men dipped it up. . . . Finally, he ordered the whiskey to

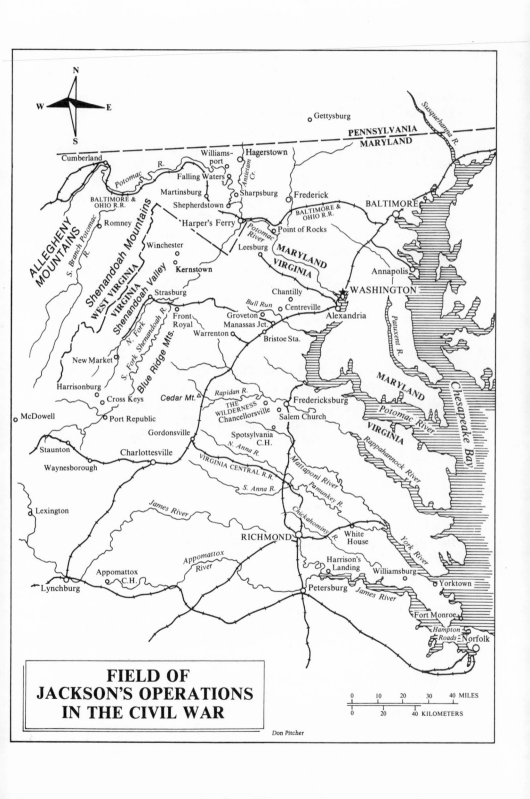

FIELD OF
JACKSON'S OPERATIONS
IN THE CIVIL WAR

Don Pitcher

be poured into the Potomac River. But still the soldiers, particularly the Kentuckians, gathered round with buckets tied to the end of ropes and caught great quantities of the disturbing element as it poured into the waters below.

Once the main supply was gone, however, a cessation of the camp's drunken revelry soon followed, and Jackson was able to set up a schedule of military instruction and drill.

Among the subordinate officers of the original command was an artillery captain, John D. Imboden, who was absent from the post when Jackson took over, having been dispatched on a military errand to Richmond. He says of his return to Harpers Ferry:

What a revolution three or four days had wrought! I could scarcely realize the change. The militia generals were all gone, and the staff had vanished. The commanding colonel and his adjutant [James W. Massie] . . . were occupying a small room in the little wayside hotel near the railroad bridge [over the Potomac].

Knowing them both, I immediately sought an interview, and delivered a letter and some papers I had brought from General Lee. Jackson and his adjutant were at a little pine table figuring upon the rolls of the troops present. They were dressed in well-worn, dingy uniforms of professors in the Virginia Military Institute, where both had recently occupied chairs. . . .

The presence of a master mind was visible in the changed condition of the camp. Perfect order reigned everywhere. Instruction in the details of military duties occupied Jackson's whole time. He urged the officers to call upon him for information about even the minutest details of duties. . . .

He was the easiest man in our army to get along with pleasantly so long as one did his duty, but as inexorable as fate in exacting the performance of it. Yet he would overlook serious faults if he saw they were the result of ignorance, and would instruct the offender in a kindly way. He was as courteous to the humblest private who sought an interview for any purpose as to the highest officer in his command. . . .

When Jackson found we were without artillery horses, he went into no red-tape correspondence with . . . Richmond, but ordered his quartermaster, Major John A. Harman, to proceed

with men to the Quaker settlements in the rich county of Lou-
doun, famous for its good horses, and buy or impress as many
as we needed. . . .

. . . J. E. B. Stuart—afterward so famous as a cavalry leader—
was commissioned lieutenant-colonel and reported to Colonel
Jackson for assignment to duty. Jackson ordered the consolida-
tion of all the cavalry companies into a battalion to be commanded by Stuart, who then appeared more like a well-grown,
manly youth than the mature man he really was.

This order was very offensive to Captain Turner Ashby, at
that time the idol of all the troopers in the field. . . . Ashby was
older than Stuart, and he thought, and we all believed, that he
was entitled to first promotion.

When not absent scouting, Ashby spent his nights with me
[on guard at the bridge at Point of Rocks, twelve miles down the
Potomac from Harpers Ferry]. . . . He told me of Jackson's
order, and that he would reply to it with his resignation. . . . I
urged him to call upon Colonel Jackson that night. . . . I believed Jackson would respect his feelings and leave his company
out of Stuart's battalion. . . .

The result of his night ride was that Jackson not only relieved
him from the obnoxious order but agreed to divide the companies between him and Stuart and to ask for his immediate
promotion, forming thus the nuclei of two regiments of
cavalry, to be filled as rapidly as new companies came to the
front. . . .

Ashby got back to Point of Rocks about two in the morning,
as happy a man as I ever saw, and completely enraptured with
Jackson.

*Imboden goes on to tell of Jackson's chief accomplishment while in
command at Harpers Ferry, one that pointed up his resourcefulness:*

From the very beginning of the war the Confederacy was
greatly in need of rolling-stock [locomotives and cars] for the
railroads. We were particularly short of locomotives, and were
without the shops to build them. Jackson, appreciating this, hit
upon a plan to obtain a good supply from the Baltimore and
Ohio road [which, operated by the Union, ran through Harpers Ferry]. Its line was double-tracked, at least from Point of

Rocks to Martinsburg, a distance of 25 or 30 miles. We had not interfered with the running of the trains. . . .

[The Confederacy did not want to anger the many Southern sympathizers who were served by the line. Even now, Jackson did not intend to do it permanent harm. He knew that the locomotives and cars he appropriated for the Confederacy would be replaced by the North, whose resources were practically infinite.]

The coal traffic from Cumberland [Maryland] was immense, as the Washington government was accumulating supplies of coal on the seaboard. These coal trains passed Harpers Ferry at all hours of the day and night, and thus furnished Jackson with a pretext for arranging a brilliant "scoop."

When he sent me to Point of Rocks [east of Harpers Ferry], he ordered Colonel [Kenton] Harper with the 5th Virginia Infantry to Martinsburg [the westerly limit of the double-tracking]. He then complained to President [J. W.] Garrett, of the Baltimore and Ohio, that the night trains, eastward bound, disturbed the repose of his camp, and requested a change of schedule that would pass all eastbound trains by Harpers Ferry between 11 and 1 o'clock in the daytime. Mr. Garrett complied, and thereafter for several days we heard the constant roar of passing trains for an hour before and an hour after noon.

But since the "empties" [from the seaboard] were sent up the road at night, Jackson again complained that the nuisance was as great as ever; and, as the road had two tracks, said he must insist that the westbound trains should pass during the same two hours as those going east. Mr. Garrett promptly complied, and we then had, for two hours every day, the liveliest railroad in America.

. . . as soon as the schedule was working at its best, Jackson sent me an order to take a force of men . . . the next day at 11 o'clock, and, letting all westbound trains pass till 12 o'clock, to permit none to go east; and at 12 o'clock to obstruct the road so that it would require several days to repair it. He ordered the reverse to be done at Martinsburg.

Thus he caught all the trains that were going east or west between those points, and these he ran [southwestward] to Winchester, thirty-two miles on the branch road, where they were safe.... The gain to our scantily stocked Virginia roads of the same gauge was invaluable.

John Gittings, once a cadet at the Virginia Military Institute and now an officer in the state of Virginia's volunteer army, had occasion to visit Harpers Ferry on military business during this period. He writes:
... Jackson was much more in his element here as an army officer than when in the professor's chair at Lexington. It seemed that the sights and sounds of war had aroused his energies. His manner had become brusque and imperative; his face was bronzed from exposure; his beard ... was worn unshorn.

Jackson was in charge at Harpers Ferry for about three and a half weeks. Then, with the command growing larger as fresh troops continued to arrive, Richmond sent General Joseph E. Johnston, one of the South's senior officers, to take over. Jackson was given command of a brigade of Virginians, the unit being made up of several infantry regiments and a battery of artillery.

(A Confederate infantry company, at top strength, held one hundred men. Regulations called for each regiment to hold ten full companies, though the regiments were often undermanned. A brigade was composed of two or more regiments, usually four or five; a division of two or more brigades, usually four; and a corps of two or more divisions, usually three.)

Jackson's Virginians—at this time called the First Brigade of the Army of the Shenandoah—were of Scotch-Irish, English, German, and Swiss descent. They had been recruited in the Shenandoah Valley and the western mountains, and all classes were represented. Men of first families, some of whom gave their calling as "gentlemen," rubbed shoulders with small-scale farmers, hunters and trappers, distillers, blacksmiths, carpenters, and clerks. The distinctions of class were minimized by the spirit of the times. These men had banded together to defend the South against what they sincerely believed to be an assault on her rights.

Much interest, of course, centered upon the brigade's commander. Says a member of the unit named D. B. Conrad:
Our senior colonel was a man who never spoke unless spoken to; never seemed to sleep; had his headquarters under a tree.... He walked about alone, the projecting visor of his blue

JACKSON in 1861.
Drawn from life.

cap concealing his features. [He wore] a bad-fitting, single-
breasted blue coat, and high boots covering the largest feet ever
seen.... His only pleasure was walking daily, at the same hour,
for his health....

... he imagined that the halves of his body did not work and
act in accord. He followed hydropathy [the "water cure"] for
dyspepsia, and after a pack in wet sheets every Sunday morning
he attended the Presbyterian church....

He ate the queerest food, and he sucked lemons constantly.... No one knew or understood him.... But he stood
very high in the estimation of all for rigid moral conduct and
the absolute faith [that could be] reposed in his word and deed.

Soon it was observed that every night there was singing and

praying under "that tree" . . . prayer meetings which, I regret to say, were attended by only a few—always, however, by his staff, who seem to have been chosen or elected because they were of his way of life.

Soon after assuming top command at Harpers Ferry, Joe Johnston found his little army in a dangerous position. In preparation for their first offensive measures in Virginia and West Virginia, Washington's war planners had sent troops into the country about fifty miles to Johnston's left (to the west) and also to the north side of the Potomac, in his front. He feared being pinched off.

Of immediate concern was the force across the river, commanded by General Robert Patterson. It was building toward a strength of 18,000 men. At present Johnston had only half that number, though he would soon have nearly 12,000.

On June 15, after burning the railroad bridge over the Potomac and destroying other property that would have been useful to the Federals, Johnston withdrew southwestward through the Valley toward Winchester. General Patterson, at Williamsport, some miles up the river from Harpers Ferry, reacted cautiously, crossing only a part of his army. Even these men were soon recalled.

On June 19 Jackson was ordered to Martinsburg, a dozen miles southwest of Williamsport, to destroy an assemblage of locomotives and cars and to observe the enemy. The destruction pained him: "It was a sad work, but I had my orders. . . . If the cost of the property could only have been expended in disseminating the gospel of the Prince of Peace, how much good might have been expected!"

General Patterson crossed the river in force at Williamsport on July 2. Jackson, with Jeb Stuart's cavalry as his "eyes," advanced with a single regiment to feel out the invasion. He had orders to fall back and report to Johnston if he made contact with substantial numbers.

Among those who took part in this mission was Private John Opie, who describes Jackson's first Civil War fight as the enlisted men saw it:

Near a little hamlet known as Hainesville [and at the site of a rural church called Falling Waters], in Berkeley County, West Virginia, about equally distant between Martinsburg and Williamsport, we came in sight of [the Federals]; but so little did our men realize that we were going into battle that they broke ranks and climbed upon the fences, that they might thereby obtain a better view.

On they came in battle array, the first army we had ever beheld; and a grand sight it was—infantry, artillery, and mounted men; their arms and accoutrements glittering in the sunlight, their colors unfurled to the breeze, their bands playing and drums beating, the officers shouting the commands, as regiments, battalions, and companies marched up and wheeled into position.

Then a battery took position and commenced firing at us. . . . The officer in command of our artillery was a pious old gentleman, an Episcopal preacher, Captain [William N.] Pendleton. . . . He named his cannon Matthew, Mark, Luke, and John. When he wished a gun to be fired, he raised his hand towards the heavens and exclaimed aloud, "May the Lord have mercy on their wicked souls! Fire!"

Our regiment, the Fifth Virginia, was deployed, and a fight immediately commenced with the enemy's sharpshooters. . . . When the first shell exploded over us, one of our company threw away his gun and fled down the pike at breakneck speed. . . . I saw a soldier fall, slightly wounded in the neck and begging to be helped up, who, when assisted to his feet, made for the rear with lightning-like rapidity—although he would not rise until assisted.

After firing at each other for about two hours, we were withdrawn and marched to Martinsburg. Neither side suffered much loss, as we were all novices in the art of killing each other. We, however, captured between forty and fifty prisoners.

It was Jeb Stuart who took the prisoners. Opie's account makes the skirmish sound simpler than it was. Committing less than 400 men, and being outnumbered about 8 to 1, Jackson conducted a masterful little action. General Patterson reported to Washington that he had been opposed by a force of 3,500!

Patterson and Johnston now took up positions and watched one another. They did not come to serious blows.

Jackson's conduct at Falling Waters won him not only official approval but also the admiration of his newest freind, Dr. Robert L. Dabney (a doctor of divinity, of course). Dabney, who was travelling with the Army of the Shenandoah as a regimental chaplain, was later to serve as Jackson's chief of staff, and was also to become one of his first biographers. Dabney says of Jackson at Falling Waters:

He was probably the only man in the detachment of infantry who had ever been under fire, but he declared that "both officers and men behaved beautifully." On the other hand, his coolness, skill, care for the lives of his men, and happy audacity [he delighted in bold maneuvers] filled them with enthusiasm. Henceforward, his influence over them was established.

Shortly after the skirmish, Colonel Jackson received the following note from Richmond:

I have the pleasure of sending you a commission of Brigadier-General in the Provisional Army; and to feel that you merit it. May your advancement increase your usefulness to the State.—Very truly, R. E. Lee.

_IV.

First Manassas

he opposing forces in the Shenandoah Valley now became part of a larger campaign. It was three months since President Lincoln had issued his first call for volunteers, and a 50,000-man army under General Irvin McDowell was assembled at Washington and just across the Potomac in Virginia. Most of these men had not yet seen a single Confederate soldier. The Northern public was becoming impatient, and newspapers everywhere raised the cry, "On to Richmond!"

The main Confederate army, about 20,000 men under General Pierre G. T. Beauregard, was gathered at Manassas Junction, twenty-five miles southwest of Washington. It was Beauregard's duty not only to block the route to Richmond but also to cover and protect the railroad junction itself. One of the tracks led northwestward through the Blue Ridge Mountains into the Shenandoah Valley. The distance between Beauregard's troops and those in the Valley was about sixty miles.

On July 16, 1861, some 35,000 men under the Union's General McDowell left their entrenched camps around Washington and started toward Manassas. The columns included infantry, artillery, and cavalry units, along with supply wagons and ambulances. Crowds of civilians—men and women on foot, on horseback, and in a variety of carriages—joined the procession. There were numerous senators and congressmen, some escorting their wives. In a holiday mood, the civilians believed they were about to witness a great Northern victory and a quick end to the rebellion.

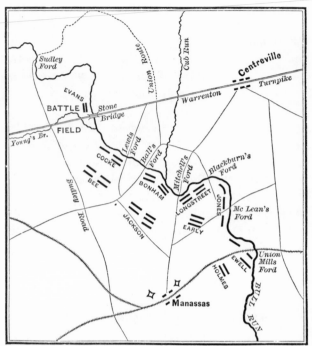

CONFEDERATE POSITIONS just prior to First Manassas. McDowell's flanking route is shown as dotted line at top center.

As for General Beauregard's army, by the evening of July 17 its seven brigades and several odd regiments were deployed for a distance of eight miles along the southwestern bank of a small stream called Bull Run. The position, which faced toward Washington, covered Manassas Junction, and its left flank lay at the Stone Bridge on the Warrenton Turnpike, the highway upon which McDowell's army was approaching.

On the eighteenth the Federals reached Centreville, about four miles from the Stone Bridge. One division, that of General Daniel Tyler, was sent forward to probe Beauregard's line, and a sharp skirmish took place at Blackburn's Ford, in the line's central section. The Federals were repulsed, and McDowell spent the next two days at Centreville preparing his main attack.

General Beauregard had meanwhile sent word to Joe Johnston in the Valley that his troops were needed at Manassas. Johnston began his march at once, with Jackson's brigade in the lead.

Jeb Stuart and his horsemen remained for a time before the Union forces and maneuvered audaciously, pretending that Johnston's whole army was still present. Stuart's acting fooled General Patterson, who had orders from Washington to watch Johnston closely, to keep him occupied, and by no means to allow him to slip away to Beauregard's support. Even as Johnston made his withdrawal, Patterson wired Washington that he was keeping the Confederate general "actively employed."

Johnston headed his columns southeast toward the Blue Ridge Mountains. According to Private John Opie, of Jackson's brigade:

We were all completely at a loss to comprehend the meaning of our retrograde movement, until a general order was read, informing us that we were marching to the relief of Beauregard at Manassas, where a great battle was imminent. At this news, the whole army set up a continuous yell. It was the first Rebel yell, which afterward became so familiar to friend and foe.

Dr. Dabney, the clergyman who had just recently become Jackson's friend, says that the men's faces were now "brightened with joy." Keeping his comments impersonal, though he was on the scene at the time, Dabney continues:

They hurried forward [with Jackson still in the lead], often at a double-quick, waded the Shenandoah River . . . ascended the Blue Ridge at Ashby's Gap, and, two hours after midnight, paused for a few hours' rest at the little village of Paris, upon the eastern slope of the mountain.

Here General Jackson turned his brigade into an enclosure occupied by a beautiful grove, and the wearied men fell prostrate upon the earth without food. In a little time an officer came to Jackson, reminded him that there were no sentries posted around his bivouac, while the men were all wrapped in sleep, and asked if some should be aroused and a guard set.

"No," replied Jackson, "let the poor fellows sleep. I will guard the camp myself."

All the remainder of the night he paced around it, or sat upon the fence, watching the slumbers of his men. An hour before daybreak, he yielded to the repeated requests of a member of his staff and relinquished the task to him. Descending from his seat upon the fence, he rolled himself upon the leaves in a corner, and in a moment was sleeping like an infant. But at the first streak of the dawn he aroused his men and resumed the march.

The brigade, with the rest of the army following, soon reached Piedmont Station, at the eastern base of the Blue Ridge. Having come thirty miles on foot, the army's infantry planned to travel the remaining thirty by rail (while the cavalry, artillery, supply wagons, and ambulances continued by road).

At the station, says Jackson's infantry soldier John Casler, "the citizens for miles around came flocking in to see us, bringing us eatables of all kinds. . . . We had a regular picnic . . . and beautiful young ladies to chat with."

Jackson reached Manassas Junction about four o'clock on Friday afternoon, July 19, and was soon deploying in a pine woods at Mitchell's Ford, near the center of Beauregard's Bull Run line. The next morning the men examined the area, which had figured in the fighting of the eighteenth, and a line of fresh graves was a sobering sight.

This was a quiet day, with more of Johnston's units arriving from the railway station and being greeted by those already deployed. Others were still far up the railroad, having been delayed by trouble with the trains. A kind of impatience prevailed along the eight-mile defense line; the men wanted to face the issue and get it settled. According to one of Jackson's soldiers, the general attitude seemed to be : "Let us get someplace where we can kill every Yankee, and then go home."

Early the following morning, Sunday, July 21, the Union's General McDowell made his move. After instructing a part of his army to demonstrate in front of the Bull Run line, he took about 13,000 men—the divisions of Generals David Hunter and Samuel P. Heintzelman—on a wide detour to his right, coming in on the line's "left shoulder."

The greater part of a brigade stationed there—six companies of South Carolinians and a battalion called the Louisiana Tigers—turned quickly to meet the attack. Woefully insufficient in numbers, they were soon joined by three or four thousand reinforcements, with General Barnard E. Bee assuming top command.

Jackson and his Virginians headed toward the sound of the firing, and Generals Johnston and Beauregard dispatched orders for other units of the line to follow. The Confederates themselves had planned to launch an attack that morning, but McDowell had beaten them to the punch.

A forced march over a wide expanse of fields and woods brought Jackson and his men at length to the base of a pine-covered ridge about two thirds of a mile behind the action. Coming down the slope were the first wounded, some hobbling along using rifles or sticks as canes, others being supported on either side by unwounded comrades, and still others *being carried in blankets serving as hammocks, a number bleeding their lives away.*

The news that these casualties imparted wasn't encouraging. The impromptu defense line, in spite of supremely heroic efforts and the competent leadership of General Bee, had been battered backward from its first position. McDowell's flanking force was too strong for it. To worsen matters, some of the Union troops who had been demonstrating on the other side of the Stone Bridge—notably a brigade under Colonel William T. Sherman—had crossed Bull Run and joined the attack.

The view that met Jackson's eye as he and his men reached the top of the ridge is described by brigade member D. B. Conrad:

... a wide clearing was discovered. A broad tableland spread out; the pine thicket ceased; and far away ... [across the next valley] was the smoke of musketry; at the bottom of the long declivity was the famous turnpike; and on the hills beyond could be seen clearly Griffin's and Ricketts' batteries [i.e., the Union artillery pieces under Captains Charles Griffin and James B. Ricketts]. In their front, to their rear, and ... on each side were long lines of blue.

Jackson halted his troops on the plateau-topped ridge, deploying them for action along the edge that was farthest from the enemy. Dr. Dabney explains:

The northern end of this ridge overlooked the Stone Bridge. Its top and western slopes ... swept down in open fields to [the] valley which divided Jackson at the moment from the advancing enemy.... Before the Confederate line were two homely cottages, with their enclosures and stables, and a country road.... The soldierly eye of Jackson, at a glance, perceived that this was the spot on which to arrest the enemy's triumph.... The swelling ridge gave his artillery a commanding elevation, whence every approach of the enemy in front could be swept with effect....

By the time Jackson was fully deployed, the crackling sound of the small-arms fighting had crept across the valley and was coming up the slope. The smoke cloud had thickened. Stray musket balls arched over the crest, but fell short of Jackson's lines. The booming guns of Griffin and Ricketts, however, reached them from time to time from their commanding positions across the valley. This fire also shattered one of the

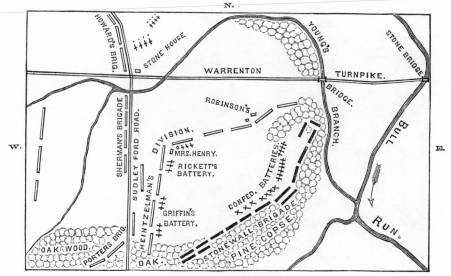

FIRST MANASSAS. The fight for the plateau.

*small houses in Jackson's front and mortally wounded its aged owner,
Mrs. Judith Henry, an invalid lying in her bed.*

*Now some of the retreating Confederates began to appear, as dim
shadows in the smoke, at the edge of the plateau. Relates Jackson's man
D. B. Conrad:*

At this time there rode up fast toward us from the front a
horse and rider.... He was ... all alone, and as he came closer,
erect and full of fire, his jet-black eyes and long hair, and ...
uniform of a general officer made him the cynosure of all. In a
strong, decided tone he inquired of the nearest aide what
troops we were and who commanded.

He was told that General Jackson, with five Virginia regiments, had just arrived, pointing to where the general stood at
the same time. The strange officer then advanced, and we of
the regimental staff crowded to where he was to hear the news
from the front. He announced himself as General B. E. Bee,
commanding South Carolina troops.

"We have been heavily engaged all the morning, and, being
overpowered ... will fall back on you as a support. The enemy
will make their appearance in a short time over the crest...."

"Then, sir, we will give them the bayonet!" was the only reply
of General Jackson.

BARNARD E. BEE.

According to Private John Casler:

It was . . . at this time that General Jackson received the name of "Stonewall," and the brigade the ever memorable name of "Stonewall Brigade."

. . . Hastening back to his men, General Bee cried enthusiastically, as he pointed to Jackson: "Look yonder! There is Jackson and his brigade standing like a stone wall. Let us determine to die here, and we will conquer. Rally behind them!"

An irreverent note is added by Private John Opie: "History does not explain this discrepancy: instead of standing, we were lying flat upon the ground by order of General Jackson."

Generals Johnston and Beauregard, having come to the front, were galloping everywhere and encouraging the retreating troops to lift their drooping flags and plant them along the line established by Jackson.

Imbued with a new spirit, the men cheered as they obeyed. Soon the line held some 6,500 men, 2,600 of whom were Jackson's.

The Federals actively engaged at this stage of the fight numbered about 11,000. Telegrams claiming victory were being sent to Washington, and the throng of civilian spectators on the heights across Bull Run were shaking hands and cheering wildly at each new roll of fire.

But the fight was only about half over. Enough Confederate troops to match McDowell's assault strength were on the way to the front. Some were coming at a fast march from the right of the original Bull Run line, while others were completing the train trip from the Blue Ridge. General Johnston soon returned to the rear to hurry the reinforcements forward. Beauregard took complete command at the front.

As the first Federals began to appear at the edge of the plateau, the attack halted to reform, and a lull ensued. It was past noon, and the sun was high and oppressive. At McDowell's order, the artillery batteries of Griffin and Ricketts forsook their heights in the rear and advanced, with their teams at a gallop, across the valley and up to the edge of the plateau with the first line of infantry.

Soon a new and more terrible battle began. As successive lines of Federals, with muskets at the ready and banners waving, advanced over the edge of the plateau, they were met by heavy artillery fire. They answered with their own artillery, as well as with musket volleys. The noise was deafening, and the earth trembled. Smoke and dust rose in great columns into the clear sky.

For a time most of the Confederates remained behind their line of artillery. Says Dr. Dabney:

... Jackson's patient infantry stood the ordeal ... lying passive behind their batteries while the plunging shot and shells of the enemy ploughed frequent gaps through their lines. He rode, the presiding genius of the storm, constantly along his lines, between the artillery and the prostrate regiments, inspiring confidence wherever he came.... His whole form was instinct with life, and while his eyes blazed with ... fire ... his countenance was clothed with a serene and assured smile.

Jackson's smile faded at least once. He happened to hear Captain John Imboden of the artillery add a blast of profanity to the general din. Jackson said nothing, but Imboden could see that he was displeased. The captain, who usually commanded only one battery, was presently placed in temporary command of the whole line. He relates:

RETREATING CONFEDERATES rallying
to form on Jackson's line.

Jackson ordered me to go from battery to battery and see that
the guns were properly aimed and the fuses cut the right
length. This was the work of but a few minutes. On returning to
the left of the line of guns, I stopped to ask General Jackson's
permission to rejoin my battery. The fight was just then hot
enough to make [the mounted general] feel well. . . .

He had a way of throwing up his left hand with the open
palm toward the person he was addressing. And as he told me
to go, he made this gesture. The air was full of flying missiles,
and as he spoke he jerked down his hand, and I saw that blood
was streaming from it.

I exclaimed, "General, you are wounded!"

He replied, as he drew a handkerchief from his breast pocket and began to bind it up, "Only a scratch—a mere scratch," and galloped away along his line.

The Union batteries of Griffin and Ricketts were in a position uncomfortably close to Jackson's left front. Jeb Stuart and his cavalrymen, who were covering Jackson's left, rode forward. Shouting as they unlimbered their carbines, handguns, and sabers, they scattered a regiment of infantry, New York's colorful Fire Zouaves, who were supporting the batteries. At the same time, Jackson's leftmost infantry regiment, the 33rd

Virginia, advanced and shot down or drove off the artillerymen and took the guns in hand. But soon a hot musket fire from the Federal lines forced the Virginians to give up their prizes and fall back.

With the Federals again on the offensive, General Beauregard ordered a charge. Dr. Dabney tells how Jackson responded:

Wheeling his guns suddenly to the rear by his right and left, he cleared away the arena before his regiments, and gave them all the signal. Riding to the [central] regiment, he cried, "Reserve your fire till they come within fifty yards, then fire and give them the bayonet; and, when you charge, yell like furies!"

Like noble hounds unleashed, his men sprang to their feet, concentrating into that moment all the pent-up energies and revenge of the hours of passive suffering, delivered one deadly volley, and dashed upon the enemy. These did not tarry to cross bayonets with them, but recoiled, broke, and fled. . . . The captured battery was recaptured, along with a regimental flag. The centre of the enemy's line of battle was pierced, and the area, for which they [the enemy] had struggled so stubbornly, cleared of their presence.

This was, for the Confederates, the critical success. . . . [Previously,] Jackson had held the enemy at bay; and the precious season had been diligently improved by the commanding generals in bringing up their reserves. . . . The decisive hour was saved, and saved chiefly by Jackson's skill and heroism.

It is true that, even when he charged the enemy's centre, their sharpshooters found an inlet through the breaches of the line upon his right and left, and almost enveloped his rear; that his brigade was partially broken and dissipated by the eagerness of its pursuit of the fugitive foe; and that their teeming numbers enabled these to return again and reoccupy a portion of the contested arena and the battery which Jackson had twice taken. But the other troops which were now at hand . . . speedily regained the lost ground [this feat taking place during another charge ordered by Beauregard].

With the afternoon now well advanced, the Federals reformed for another attack. But their chance for victory had passed. More Confederate reserves were arriving, both from the right of the original Bull Run line and from the railroad junction—these latter being the last of the troops from the Valley, under E. Kirby Smith.

As General Smith led his men around the extreme left of the Confederate line in preparation to striking McDowell's right, Jackson's troops at first believed them to be Federals. Relates Private Opie:

At this moment, men began to cry out, "We are flanked! We are flanked!" pointing to the left.

In full view, about a mile from us, we saw several regiments wheeling into line. We could not determine at that distance to which side they belonged.... General Jackson quickly dispatched several mounted men to learn who they were, and to report as speedily as possible.

We waited for a few minutes in suspense, when the men came galloping back, yelling at the top of their voices, "It is Kirby Smith! It is Kirby Smith!"

Whereupon General Jackson sent his aides to the different colonels of regiments with orders to charge at once and preserve the alignment. We sprang forward, five crack Virginia regiments, with a yell that almost shook the universe. Simultaneously, Kirby Smith ... [followed by a brigade under Jubal Early, newly arrived from the other end of the Bull Run line] was plunging with fixed bayonets into the right flank of the enemy.

For a brief time, Opie goes on to say, the Federals fired back briskly. Then:

... regardless of the threats and expostulations of their officers, they broke ranks, and—many of them divesting themselves of all impedimenta, such as guns, canteens, and cartridge belts—all sought safety in flight....

Soon all of the Federals were back across Bull Run. Dr. Dabney relates that

Cannon, small arms, standards, were deserted. The great causeway from the Stone Bridge to Centreville was one surging and maddened mass of men, horses, artillery, and baggage, amidst which the gay equipages [i.e., carriages] of the amateur spectators of the carnage, male and female, were crushed like shells; while the Confederate cavalry scourged their flanks, and [Captain Del] Kemper's field-battery, from behind, pressed them like a Nemesis....

In this pursuit Jackson took no share, except to plant a battery upon a rising ground at his rear, whence he could speed the flight of the enemy with some parting shots. He retired then to seek relief for [the] painful wound in the hand . . . while his officers collected their wearied and shattered men, and ministered to their disabled comrades.

Along a little rivulet, fringed with willows, which ran behind the hill that [had] received the farthest cannon shot of the enemy, many hundreds of wounded Confederates were gathered, with many more of shameless stragglers who had deserted the field under the pretext of assisting disabled comrades.

. . . the surgeons were busy here, under the grateful shade, plying their repulsive but benevolent task, and the greensward was strewn for half a mile with men writhing in every form of suffering, and the corpses of those just dead.

Here Jackson found the medical director [Dr. Hunter McGuire] and the surgeons of his brigade. . . . Several surgeons now gathered around to examine him, but he refused their services, saying, "No, I can wait; my wound is a trifle; attend first to these poor fellows." And . . . he sat by upon the grass holding up his bloody hand, evidently suffering acute pain, but with a quiet smile on his face.

After the common soldiers were attended to, he submitted to . . . examination, and, as they passed judgment upon the nature of the wound, he looked intently from one speaker to another, while all, except their chief, concurred in declaring that one finger at least must be removed immediately.

Turning to him, he said, "Dr. McGuire, what is your opinion?"

He answered, "General, if we attempt to save the finger, the cure will be more painful; but if this were my hand I should make the experiment."

His only reply was to lay the mangled hand in Dr. McGuire's, with a calm and decisive motion, saying, "Doctor . . . you dress it."

. . . While he was at this place, the President of the Confederate States [Jefferson Davis], with a brilliant staff, galloped by towards the battlefield. . . . General Jackson arose . . . and exhorted the men to give him a lusty cheer. . . .

The stimulation of the moment caused Jackson to lose his customary reticence. According to Dr. McGuire:

He... took off his cap and cried, "We have whipped them—they ran like sheep! Give me ten thousand men and I will take Washington City tomorrow!"

No such effort was to be made. Even the pursuit of the fleeing troops (who were headed back to the capital) was shortly abandoned, since the Confederates were almost as disorganized by their victory as the Federals were by their defeat.

The results of the battle were that the Confederates captured a great deal of valuable equipment, that Virginia was delivered from the immediate danger of invasion, and that the North was sobered regarding the task of saving the Union. The battle cost the Federal army nearly 3,000 men in killed, wounded, captured, and missing; the Confederates lost about 2,000. Adds Dr. Dabney:

The portion of the Confederate loss borne by Jackson's brigade was the best evidence of the character of their resistance.... Out of less than 2,700 men present it lost 112 killed and 393 wounded....

Had the enemy overpowered [the] brigade and occupied the eminence which was the key of the Confederate position, or had they not been held at bay until forces could be assembled to cope with them, no other [successful] stand could have been made.... In this sense Jackson may be said to have won the First Battle of Manassas.

Jackson's wife says that he gave credit for the victory to "God alone." She quotes a letter he wrote her on the morning after the battle:

Although under a heavy fire for several continuous hours, I received only one wound, the breaking of the longest finger of my left hand.... My horse was wounded but not killed. [My] coat got an ugly wound near the hip, but my servant, who is very handy, has so far repaired it that it doesn't show very much....

Whilst great credit is due to other parts of our gallant army, God made my brigade more instrumental than any other in repulsing the main attack. This is for your information only— say nothing about it. Let others speak praise, not myself.

Jackson wrote another letter at the same sitting, this one to his pastor in Lexington. Mary Anna relates:

A day or two after the battle . . . before the news of the victory had reached Lexington in authentic form, the post-office was thronged with people awaiting with intense interest the opening of the mail. Soon a letter was handed to the Rev. Dr. White, who immediately recognized the well-known superscription of his deacon soldier, and exclaimed to the eager and expectant group around him: "Now we shall know all the facts." Upon opening it, the bulletin read thus:

"My dear pastor—In my tent last night, after a fatiguing day's service, I remembered that I had failed to send you my contribution for our colored Sunday-school. Enclosed you will find my check for that object, which please acknowledge at your earliest convenience, and oblige yours faithfully, T. J. Jackson."

V.

The Valley Campaign

Jackson's camp, after First Manassas, was located near Centreville. In the beginning, as Dr. McGuire had predicted, the general's injury was very bothersome. On the third morning after the battle, artilleryman John Imboden rode from his own tent to Jackson's to learn how he was faring:

Although it was barely sunrise, he was out under the trees, bathing the hand with spring water. It was much swollen and very painful, but he bore himself stoically. . . .

Of course, the battle was the only topic discussed at breakfast. I remarked . . . "General, how is it that you can keep so cool and appear so utterly insensible to danger in such a storm of shell and bullets as rained about you when your hand was hit?"

He instantly became grave and reverential in his manner, and answered in a low tone of great earnestness: "Captain, my religious belief teaches me to feel as safe in battle as in bed. God has fixed the time for my death. I do not concern myself about *that,* but to be always ready, no matter when it may overtake me."

He added, after a pause, looking me full in the face: "Captain, that is the way all men should live, and then all would be equally brave."

I felt that this last remark was intended as a rebuke for my profanity . . . on the field . . . and I apologized.

He heard me, and simply said, "Nothing can justify profanity."

As for Jackson's finger, it would eventually become sound again. His general health, as his friend Dr. Dabney explains, was good at this time:

The life in the open air proved a cordial to his feeble constitution. Every appearance of the scholastic languor vanished from his face, his eye grew bright, and its vision, so long enfeebled, was so fully restored that thenceforward it endured, by night and by day, all the labors of his burdensome correspondence and the business of his command. His cheek grew ruddy and his frame expanded, so that . . . he appeared a new man.

Jackson gave due credit to the vigorous outdoor life for his improved health, but he retained some of his curious beliefs. He continued to suck lemons, for he considered the juice to be a digestive aid. This belief wasn't too hard for his men to accept, but tongues clicked behind his back when he was heard to say that he never peppered his food because this caused a weakness in his left leg.

As the weeks passed, Jackson fretted because Richmond made no plans to carry the war into Northern territory. He spent the time training his troops.

About two months after First Manassas, in September 1861, Mary Anna came up from North Carolina to pay Jackson a visit. She relates:

It was a grand spectacle to view . . . the encampment of that splendid Stonewall Brigade, especially at night, when the campfires were lighted. . . . General Jackson was justly proud of his brigade. . . .

He took me over the battlefield. . . . Much of the debris . . . still remained. The old Henry house was riddled with shot and shell. The carcasses of the horses, and even some of the bones of the poor human victims, were to be seen. . . .

All was quiet in the army during my visit. . . . We had a nice room in a kind, obliging family named Utterbach, and I took my meals with him and his staff at their mess table under the trees. . . .

But all things have to come to an end in this fleeting world, and . . . all too soon . . . I was sent back sorrowfully to North Carolina.

Jackson was promoted to major general that autumn, and on November 4 he received orders to proceed to Winchester, in the Shenandoah Valley, to take command of "the military district of the Northern frontier, between the Blue Ridge and the Allegheny Mountains." He was to go alone, and just before leaving he called his brigade together and gave them a brief farewell address. As he closed, the men made the countryside ring with their cheers. According to Private John Opie:

... "Old Jack" rode rapidly away to conceal his emotion. He looked as if he would tumble from his horse, as he was an extremely awkward rider. We were very much grieved at the loss of our commander, but soon received unexpected orders to join him in the Valley.

Mary Anna also joined him, delighted that another visit had become possible so soon:

My husband was fortunate enough to engage board for us both with the Rev. J. R. Graham.... Winchester was rich in happy homes and pleasant people ... and the extreme kindness and appreciation shown to General Jackson by all, bound us both to them ... closely and warmly....

A special friend was Mrs. Anne Tucker Magill, an elderly woman with "the richest vein of humor." Mary Anna says that Mrs. Magill helped to create "a very amusing scene" in the Graham living room:

A number of visitors, including several young officers, were spending the evening, and as they were about breaking up, Mrs. Magill and a young captain of artillery began to fight a most ridiculous battle—the captain seizing a chair as his cannon and pointing its back at Mrs. Magill. The fun became contagious, and soon everybody in the room took sides, drawing out the chairs as pieces of artillery, amid such noise and laughter that General Jackson, who was in his room upstairs, came down to see what it was all about. Taking in at a glance the broad humor of the occasion, he said sharply: "Captain Marye, when the engagement is over, you will send in an official report!"

In spite of a shortage of troops, Jackson did some campaigning that winter. With Winchester located near the northern end of the Valley, he was less than fifty miles from several detachments of Federals. On January 1, 1862, he undertook what was to become known as the

Romney Expedition, which began as a movement northward toward the Potomac River.

"The weather," explains artillery officer John Imboden,

set in to be very inclement... with snow, rain, sleet, high winds, and intense cold. Many in Jackson's command were opposed to the expedition, and as it resulted in nothing of much military importance, but was attended with great suffering on the part of his troops, nothing but the confidence he had won by his previous services saved him from personal ruin. . . .

In that terrible winter's march and exposure, Jackson endured all that any private was exposed to. One morning, near Bath, some of his men, having crawled out from under their snow-laden blankets, half frozen, were cursing him as the cause of their sufferings. He lay close by under a tree, also snowed under, and heard all this; and, without noticing it, presently crawled out, too, and shaking the snow off, made some jocular remark to the nearest men, who had no idea he had ridden up in the night and lain down amongst them.

Many of the expedition's members blamed their troubles on the Yankees. One man went so far as to say he wished they were all in hell. Another protested, saying that Jackson would only follow them there!

The expedition drove many of the Federals out of the district, at least temporarily (capturing their post at Romney, about forty miles northwest of Winchester), and also did considerable damage to railway, canal, and telegraph communications. So, in spite of the discord in the ranks and the doubts that arose in Richmond, Jackson was moderately satisfied as things came to a close. He was now eager to get back to Winchester and his wife. She relates: ⌐

. . . General Jackson returned from Romney to Winchester so full of animation and high spirits, galloping along on his little sorrel with such speed through the mud and slush, that one of his elder staff-officers laughingly said to him: "Well, general, *I* am not so anxious to see Mrs. Jackson as to break my neck keeping up with you, and with your permission I shall fall back and take it more leisurely."

. . . General Jackson, with the younger members of the staff, rode the whole forty miles in one short winter day. After going to a hotel and divesting himself of the mud which had bespattered him . . . he rang the doorbell . . . and in another moment he came bounding into the sitting room as joyous and fresh as a schoolboy....

As soon as the first glad greetings were over ... he glanced around the room, and was so impressed with the cosy and cheerful aspect of Mr. Graham's fireside, as we all sat round it that winter evening, that he exclaimed: "Oh, this is the very essence of comfort!"

On the Romney Expedition, trouble had developed between Jackson and one of his infantry commanders, General William W. Loring, who wasn't able to keep all his men moving through the harsh weather. Jackson had no patience with officers who failed to carry out his orders with the utmost dispatch and to the very letter. He was apt to turn a deaf ear to explanations for failure, even when they were reasonable.

As the expedition ended, Jackson had assigned Loring and his command the task of occupying Romney for the winter. It was an isolated and uncomfortable post, and Loring and his officers claimed that it wasn't worth their sacrifices, that it could not be defended against attack. Loring soon allowed a group of his officers to go over Jackson's head and complain to Secretary of War Judah P. Benjamin in Richmond. The Secretary ordered Jackson to recall the command to Winchester.

One of Jackson's officers, Henry Kyd Douglas, tells what happened after the order was obeyed:

General Jackson promptly resigned, and there was at once a storm. The army became excited, the people of the Valley indignant [Jackson, their protector against the Federals, was one of their own]. Jackson was cool and immovable. The governor of Virginia interposed, and the Secretary of War yielded. Loring was send elsewhere, and Jackson resumed his command, and this was the last time the War Department ever undertook to interfere with his proper authority.

In early March, with the spring campaign about to begin, Jackson reluctantly put Mary Anna aboard a train for North Carolina. During the trip she overheard a woman ask a Confederate officer what he thought of "Old Stonewall." The answer was gratifying: "I have the most implicit confidence in him, madam.... I would follow him anywhere." Mary Anna would not see her husband again for thirteen months.

In the new campaign, Jackson's work was tied in with a second Federal advance from Washington to Richmond. Jackson's immediate opponent was General Nathaniel P. Banks, who controlled Harpers Ferry, on the Potomac River about twenty-five miles northeast of Winchester. Banks, with about 38,000 men, was covering the "back door" to Washington, the city lying some fifty miles southeastward along the river.

Banks had orders to drive Jackson from the valley and then move eastward to Washington to help protect it and to cooperate while a great army under General George B. McClellan made the Richmond attack. This army was to sail from Washington down the Potomac and the Chesapeake Bay, disembarking at the tip of the Virginia Peninsula, the length of land between the York and James rivers. Richmond was about sixty-five miles northwest of the disembarkation point.

Jackson, having only about 5,000 men at this time, evacuated Winchester and retreated southward through the Valley. General Banks occupied Winchester. He was so certain that Jackson was making a complete withdrawal from the Valley that he soon dispatched a large part of his army toward Washington. Jackson had received orders from Richmond to try to prevent this. The more Federals he could keep busy in the Valley, the fewer would be available for McClellan's campaign against Richmond.

When Banks's troops abandoned the pursuit of Jackson about forty miles south of Winchester and turned back, Jackson turned back, too. He hurled 3,000 men against 7,000 of the enemy at Kernstown on March 23. In the words of Private John Casler:

General Jackson ... repeatedly charged them, but was driven back, and finally had to give up the field and retreat. Darkness was all that saved us.... We continued to fall back in good order to the south side of Cedar Creek, Ashby's cavalry holding the enemy in check. They did not appear very anxious for another fight.... The citizens who gathered up our dead, and buried them, reported eighty-three dead on the field. A greater portion of the wounded fell into the enemy's hands....

Though Jackson was defeated, his object was accomplished. Banks, feeling that Jackson would not have swung northward to attack unless he had been strongly reinforced, recalled the troops he had sent toward Washington. At the same time, President Lincoln decided that Washington needed extra protection and therefore withheld General Irvin

McDowell's corps from McClellan's army. The President also sent a division of reinforcements to Union-controlled West Virginia, over the mountains to Jackson's left.

Jackson's tactical defeat at Kernstown, then, turned out to be a great strategic victory. McClellan's campaign against Richmond, just beginning at the Peninsula's tip, was considerably weakened.

General Banks, with nearly 20,000 men, again pressed southward to drive Jackson from the Valley. Though getting only minor resistance from Jackson's rear guard under Ashby, Banks took several weeks to reach Harrisonburg, about seventy miles southwest of Winchester. At the same time, Union General John C. Frémont, who commanded in West Virginia, had begun sending troops toward the Shenandoah Mountains in the Valley's western section, these troops intending to cross over at a point southwest of Harrisonburg in order to form a junction with Banks.

By this time Jackson had been reinforced; he had about 17,000 men. But a junction of Frémont and Banks would give the Federals a total of 35,000. Jackson determined to prevent the junction.

It was the end of April 1862. Jackson, as one Union officer later lamented, "assumed the offensive and began that succession of movements which ended in the complete derangement of the Union plans in Virginia—on the Peninsula as well as in the Shenandoah."

Jackson wasn't without advantages as he undertook this offensive. Having lived in the Valley, he was well-acquainted with it. Said one of his officers: "He knows all the distances, all the roads, even to cowpaths through the woods and goat-tracks along the hills." Moreover, thanks to his cavalry scouts, to spies, and to friendly civilians, Jackson always knew what the enemy was doing.

Leaving a part of his force in a threatening position in front of Banks, Jackson took the rest on a march eastward, as though beginning a general retreat upon Richmond. Contending with heavy rains and deep mire, he passed through a gap in the Blue Ridge to Mechum's River Station, on the Virginia Central Railroad. His men, many of whom were natives of the Valley, were sad over the seeming abandonment of their relatives and friends. But the trains they boarded headed back through the Blue Ridge, depositing them at Staunton, in the Valley's center. The surprised citizens greeted them joyfully.

By a rapid march westward over the Shenandoah Mountains to nearby Bull Pasture Mountain, Jackson met the first of Frémont's troops, led by General Robert H. Milroy, coming from West Virginia to join Banks. On

JOHN C. FRÉMONT.

May 8, near the village of McDowell, 4,000 of Jackson's men clashed with 2,500 Federals. The outnumbered Federals fought well, finally withdrawing from the field in good order under cover of darkness.

Relates Dr. Dabney, who was now serving as Jackson's chief of staff:

By nine o'clock, the roar of the struggle had passed away, and the green battlefield reposed under the starlight.... Detachments of soldiers were silently exploring the ground for their wounded comrades, while the tired troops were slowly filing off to their bivouac.

At midnight the last sufferer had been removed and the last picket posted; and then only did General Jackson turn... [toward] a farmhouse at the eastern base of the mountain. The Valley of McDowell lay beneath him.... The campfires of the Federals blazed ostentatiously in long and regular lines....

DETAIL FROM A MAP of Virginia and West Virginia showing Jackson's route during the Valley Campaign. From Staunton (lower left), he marched northwestward and defeated Frémont's van near McDowell on May 8. Turning back and swinging northward by way of Harrisonburg, New Market, and Luray, he hit Banks at Front Royal on May 23. Banks retreated toward Winchester, was defeated there on May 25. Map does not show that Banks continued his retreat northward and crossed the Potomac River into Maryland, with Jackson following as far as the river. With his rear threatened by Frémont and McDowell, Jackson turned back to Winchester and began retreating southward by way of Strasburg and Harrisonburg. He struck Frémont at Cross Keys on June 8, and McDowell's van, led by Shields, at Port Republic on June 9. Ten days later he began marching toward Richmond by way of Gordonsville.

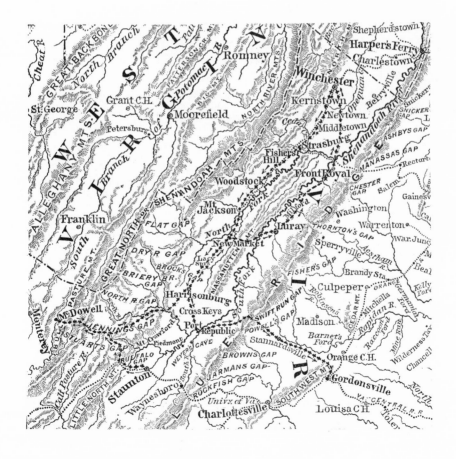

At one o'clock A.M. the General reached his quarters and threw himself upon a bed. When his faithful servant, knowing that he had eaten nothing since morning, came with food, he said, "I want none; nothing but sleep."

... The dawn found him in the saddle and ascending the mountain again. When he reached the crest of the battlefield, he saw the vale beneath him deserted. The foe had decamped in the night, leaving their dead, and partially destroying their camp equipage and stores.

Frémont's move to join Banks had been frustrated, the advance troops retreating back toward West Virginia. Jackson organized a pursuit through the wooded country, the way being marked by fresh graves and broken-down supply wagons. Three days later the pursuers were stopped by a great forest fire set by the enemy's rear guard, an expedient that Jackson couldn't help but admire.

Since the last part of the pursuit was made on a Sunday, Jackson set aside half of Monday for divine services. Prayer, of course, was very much a part of Jackson's campaigning. For private prayer, he often went off by himself in the woods. It was suspected by his men that he also prayed silently while walking around in camp, for he was once heard to say that he could find nothing in the Scriptures that forbade one to pray with his eyes open.

Private John Opie noted that Jackson took time for prayer even during busy moments on the battlefield:

General Jackson would often sit upon his horse, in the hottest fire, oblivious to the existence of danger, his eyes lifted towards the heavens.... I often wondered what he asked for in his petitions.... It was certainly not Scriptural to pray for the annihilation of his enemies, yet, under the circumstances, he must have desired it.

In both North and South, Jackson's name was now becoming a very familiar one. The South considered him a true hero of the cause. But, upon seeing him for the first time, most people were disappointed. Writes Confederate officer John E. Cooke:

The outward appearance of the famous leader [who was now thirty-eight years old] was not imposing.... He wore an old sun-embrowned coat ... now almost out at [the] elbows.... The remainder of the General's costume was as much discolored as

JACKSON at prayer
during the Valley
Campaign.

the coat. He wore cavalry boots reaching to the knee, and his
head was surmounted by an old cap, more faded than all; the
sun had turned it quite yellow indeed, and it tilted forward so
far over the wearer's forehead that he was compelled to raise
his chin in the air in order to look under the rim.

His horse was not a "fiery steed," pawing and ready to dart
forward ... but ... a horse of astonishing equanimity, who
seemed to give himself no concern on any subject, and calmly
moved about, like his master, careless of cannonball or bullet in
the hottest moments of battle.

*In a scuffed haversack attached to Little Sorrel's saddle, most observers
were unaware, were three well-worn books: a Bible, a copy of Napo-*

leon's Maxims of War, *and a dictionary—the last for Jackson's use
when he wrote his letters and reports; in spite of his considerable education and culture, he was an uncertain speller.*

*Jackson was becoming ever more popular with the men who served
under him, this in spite of his severe demands on them and the rigidity
of his discipline—which carried so far as to place an occasional man
before a firing squad.*

Again in the words of John Cooke:

Jackson's appearance and manners ... were such as conciliate
a familiar, humorous liking. His ... dress, his odd ways, his
kindly, simple manner, his habit of sitting down and eating with
his men; his indifference whether his bed were in a comfortable
headquarter tent, on a camp couch, or in a fence corner with no
shelter from the rain but his cloak; his abstemiousness, fairness,
honesty, simplicity; his never-failing regard for the comfort
and the feelings of the private soldier; his oddities, eccentricities, and originalities—all were an unfailing provocative to
liking, and endeared him to his men.

Troops are charmed when there is anything in the personal
character of a great leader to "make fun of." Admiration of his
genius then becomes enthusiasm for his person. Jackson had
aroused this enthusiasm in his men—and it was a weapon with
which he struck hard.

*President Lincoln had been watching events in the Valley very closely.
He was informed by General McClellan, then moving slowly up the
Peninsula toward Richmond, that it wasn't likely Jackson had any
designs on Washington, that his whole purpose was probably the disrup-
tion of the Richmond campaign. McClellan asked Lincoln for reinforcements. Consequently Banks was again ordered to send some of his
Valley units eastward. They were to join General McDowell, who was to
march southward to link up with McClellan.*

*Jackson, with the approval of General Lee in Richmond, moved to
thwart the plan. He gathered all of his forces to march against Banks,
who, now outnumbered, had withdrawn northward and set up a defense
line eastward through the Valley from Strasburg to Front Royal, the
line being about twenty miles south of Winchester and some forty miles
from Harpers Ferry on the Potomac.*

*Jackson hurried toward Front Royal, which held only a small garri-
son. According to artilleryman John Imboden:*

He sometimes made thirty miles in twenty-four hours with his entire army, thus gaining for his infantry the sobriquet of "Jackson's foot cavalry." [These men claimed that Jackson always marched at dawn, except when he started the night before.]

Very early in the afternoon of May 23d he struck Front Royal. The surprise was complete and disastrous to the enemy, who . . . fled [northward] toward Winchester . . . with Jackson at their heels. . . .

News of this disaster reached Banks at Strasburg [to the west], by which he learned that Jackson was rapidly gaining his rear . . . so he . . . set out with all haste toward Winchester; but, enroute . . . Jackson struck his flank, inflicting heavy loss and making large captures of property . . . besides a large number of prisoners.

Jackson now chased Banks's fleeing army to Winchester, where the latter made a stand; but after a sharp engagement . . . on the 25th he fled again, not halting till he had crossed the Potomac, congratulating himself and his Government . . . that his army was at last safe in Maryland.

While Jackson was driving Banks northward, the wildest excitement seized Washington. General McDowell, who had started southward to join McClellan, was turned back and ordered to take 20,000 of his men westward to the Valley. Frémont, in West Virginia, was again ordered to press a column eastward over the Shenandoah Mountains. This column was 15,000 strong. Additional troops, some of them militiamen called up for the emergency, joined the remnant of Banks's army just north of the Potomac.

Jackson remained south of the river, demonstrating as though he planned to cross. His command at this time numbered no more than 15,000.

President Lincoln had hatched a plan by which he hoped to end his troubles with Jackson. The western column under Frémont and the eastern column under McDowell were to march toward a junction in the Valley behind Jackson, forcing him to turn back from the Potomac to meet them. His destruction was supposed to follow.

How Jackson reacted to the crisis is explained by William Allan, one of his supply officers:

Keeping up his demonstrations until the last moment—until,

indeed, the head of McDowell's column is already crossing the Blue Ridge . . . [and Frémont is closing in from West Virginia] at a point nearly fifty miles in his rear, he, by a forced march of a day and a half, traverses this distance . . . and places himself at Strasburg.

Here he keeps Frémont at bay until his long train of prisoners and captured stores has passed through in safety. . . . Then he [retreats southward] before Frémont, while by burning successively the bridges over the Main Fork of the Shenandoah [which parallels his course on his left, or to the east], he destroys all cooperation between his two pursuers.

The advance units of McDowell's column, led by General James Shields, were lagging at this time and could offer no resistance to Jackson's bridge burning. William Allan continues:

Arrived at a point where he thinks there is no further need for retreat, he turns off from Harrisonburg to Port Republic, seizes the only bridge left south of Front Royal . . . and takes a position which enables him to fight his adversaries in succession, while they cannot succor each other.

By wonderful celerity and daring, he has extricated himself from the dangers which a week before gathered around him. . . . In a day or two he must have been overwhelmed. Now he has left the great mass of these troops [strung out] fifty miles in the rear.

Frémont alone is for the moment within reach. [At Cross Keys on June 8] Jackson deals him a staggering blow; and next morning, withdrawing suddenly from his front and destroying the bridge to prevent his following, attacks the advance brigades of Shields [at Port Republic] and completely defeats them, driving them several miles from the battlefield.

Jackson's success against Frémont was marred by the loss of brilliant cavalry commander Turner Ashby, a victim of Federal musket fire.

With the twin victories of Cross Keys and Port Republic, which put an end to the Union pursuit, Jackson's Valley Campaign came to a close.

The campaign was to enter history, on an international level, as a military masterpiece. After his defeat at Kernstown, Jackson had been consistently victorious. During a period of forty days he had marched

400 miles, confused the commanders of three armies, won five battles, killed or wounded 3,500 Federals and captured another 3,500, along with an immense quantity of valuable military equipment—and he had managed to do all this with the moderate loss of about 3,000 men in killed, wounded, and captured.

Some of the reasons for this remarkable record are given by John Imboden:

Jackson's military operations were always unexpected and mysterious. In my personal intercourse with him . . . he often said there were two things never to be lost sight of by a military commander: "Always mystify, mislead, and surprise the enemy, if possible; and when you strike and overcome him, never let up in the pursuit so long as your men have strength to follow; for an army routed, if hotly pursued, becomes panic-stricken, and can then be destroyed by half their number.

"The other rule is, never fight against heavy odds, if by any possible manoeuvring you can hurl your own force on only a part—and that the weakest part—of your enemy and crush it. Such tactics will win every time, and a small army may thus destroy a large one in detail; and repeated victory will make it invincible."

His celerity of movement was a simple matter. He never broke down his men by too-long-continued marching. He rested the whole column very often, but only for a few minutes at a time. . . . He liked to see the men lie down flat on the ground to rest, and would say, "A man rests all over when he lies down."

Ten days after his concluding victory, Jackson manged to perform still another feat of movement. Without letting the Federals know what he was up to, he marched his troops southeastward from the Valley, his destination Richmond.

None of the Federals that Jackson had fought in the Valley would get to the Richmond area to help McClellan, but Jackson would get there to help Lee.

~VI.

The Seven Days

Jackson had been further reinforced, and his command now numbered about 20,000. General John B. Hood and his brigade of Texans were among the newest arrivals.

"These men," explains an unnamed newspaper correspondent,
... had never seen Jackson.... As the movement [toward Richmond] was of the highest importance, it was necessary to keep it as secret as possible. Orders were accordingly issued to the men to refuse to give information of any kind ... on the route. ...

On the second day of the march, General Jackson saw two of Hood's men leave the ranks and start for a cherry tree in the neighboring field. Riding up to them, he demanded sternly, "Where are you going?"

"I don't know," replied one of the men ... not knowing to whom he was speaking.

"What is your name?"

"I don't know."

"What regiment do you belong to?"

"I don't know."

"What does this mean?" asked the general, turning to the other man, who stood by silently.

"Why, you see," replied the soldier, "Old Stonewall gave orders yesterday that we are not to know anything ... and we mean to obey him."

70

The general smiled . . . and sent the men back to their regiment.

On June 25, 1862, Jackson's column reached Ashland, about fifteen miles north of Richmond. The situation at the Confederate capital was critical. Union General McClellan, with 100,000 men, had approached to within a few miles of its defenses. His entrenchments spanned a fifteen-mile front around the city's northeast side, along the line of the Chickahominy River. His right lay along the north bank of the river, his left along the south.

Richmond's defenses held about 70,000 men. On May 31, a part of these forces had attacked the wing of McClellan's army entrenched south of the river. The Confederates were repulsed, the battle becoming known as Fair Oaks, or Seven Pines.

The only bright spot in the situation was that in mid-June Jeb Stuart and his horsemen had ridden entirely around McClellan's army, raiding as they went, and had set him worrying about his communications with his supply depot at White House, on the Pamunkey River fifteen miles to the east.

Unknown to General Lee, but greatly to his advantage, McClellan had other worries. He had come to believe that Lee had about 200,000 men and that the Union army was in grave danger. McClellan, though in some ways a good leader, was not an aggressive fighter. He was quick to accept exaggerated reports of the enemy's strength; he allowed himself to be ruled by his apprehensions; and he always operated with extreme caution.

Now, while McClellan hesitated, the Confederates planned another attack. Leaving Richmond only lightly defended, Lee would steal northward across the Chickahominy, turn right, and strike that part of McClellan's army entrenched along the north bank. Lee hoped that this would compel McClellan to turn from Richmond and move eastward toward his supply depot at White House.

Lee's plan resulted in the Battle of Mechanicsville, or Beaver Dam Creek (June 26). The Confederates suffered another repulse, due to the fact that Jackson, scheduled to march southward from Ashland and hit McClellan's right flank, failed to arrive. He was now in unfamiliar country, and the Federals delayed him by skirmishing with his van, and by felling trees and destroying bridges along his route.

Before dawn of the following day, General McClellan withdrew his victorious troops eastward along the north side of the Chickahominy until they were directly across the river from his main body, still in its

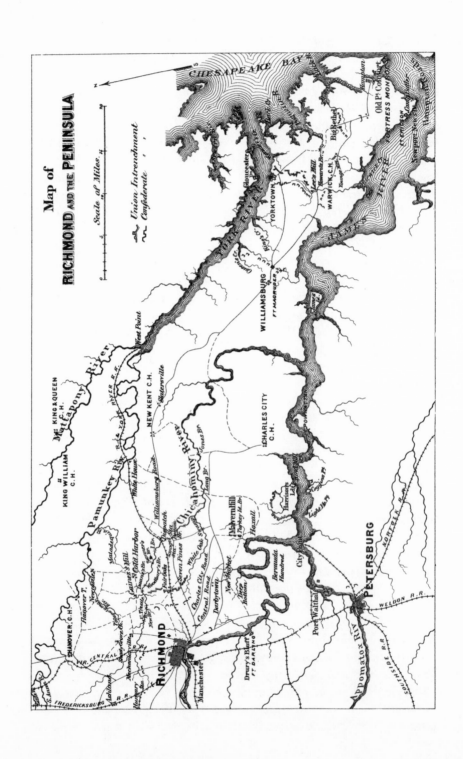

Map of
RICHMOND AND THE PENINSULA

Scale of Miles.

Union Intrenchment
Confederate   "

original position. Here, near Gaines's Mill and Old Cold Harbor, the withdrawn forces set up another defense line, a semicircle facing to the northwest, its left flank near the river and its right flank about two miles from it. The men's backs were toward the river and toward good bridge connections with the main body.

Incredibly, McClellan was planning to make a general retreat from Richmond. Though he had won his first battles near the city, he still believed that Lee had twice as many men as he had. Actually McClellan would still outnumber Lee when Jackson arrived.

McClellan did not plan to retreat eastward to White House; he was looking southward across the Peninsula to Harrison's Landing, on the James River about twenty miles southeast of Richmond. Here he planned to establish a new supply base under the guns of a Federal fleet. From this point he expected to make a second advance against Richmond—after he had talked President Lincoln into sending him 100,000 reinforcements!

To cover the evacuation of his supplies from White House, McClellan had to fight another battle north of the Chickahominy. On the afternoon of the same day that his new defense line was established (June 27), Lee moved to attack it. Jackson wasn't on hand as the Battle of Gaines's Mill began, but was marching toward the Union right. During two hours of bitter fighting, the Confederates made no gains. Jackson approached the field about four o'clock, his participation in the battle beginning with a novel incident. Relates Confederate General D. H. Hill:

Riding in advance of his skirmish line through the swamp, attended by a few staff officers, General Jackson found himself in the presence of fifteen or twenty Federal soldiers on outpost duty. He judged it the part of prudence to assume the offensive and charge upon them before they fired upon him.

Ordered by Jackson to surrender, the surprised Federals made no resistance. As they were escorted to the rear by some of Jackson's soldiers, they were seen by Confederate Major T. O. Chestney and several other officers who happened to be moving forward along the same route. Says Chestney:

A tall fellow at the head of the little party drew special attention to himself by singing out to us at the top of his voice ... "Gentlemen, we had the honor of being captured by Stonewall Jackson himself," a statement which he repeated with evident pride all along the line, as our men tramped past.

UNION SOLDIER making the boast that he and his comrades "had the honor of being captured by Stonewall Jackson himself."

As Jackson's units took their place at the front—most going to the Confederate left but some being sent to reinforce other parts of the line—the men chanted, "Stonewall Jackson! Stonewall Jackson!" And among the original fighters, who were by this time badly bloodied and doubtful of success, a new hope rose, with the men crying, "Jackson is here! Jackson is here!"

After placing his units, Jackson, astride his sorrel, took up a position at Old Cold Harbor House, at the left of the Confederate line. He was seen there by John Cooke, on the battlefield as a messenger:

He was sucking a lemon, and ... listening ... to the continuous roar of musketry from the woods ... and, riding slowly to and fro across the fields, he was subjected to a heavy fire of shell, which he appeared wholly unconscious of....

... the moment had now come when the Federal positions must be carried, or the day be lost.... Jackson's men... must... struggle through swamps, in which the feet sunk at every step... clamber over the enemy's abatis of felled trees, with the bows lopped and sharpened... penetrate undergrowth, wade through deep ditches, and charge masked batteries which were vomiting masses of shell and canister in their faces [canister being a type of ammunition that turned a cannon into a giant shotgun]....

... the banks of the Chickahominy near Powhite Creek were enveloped in a vast lurid canopy [a combination of the battlefield's rising smoke and reflections from a red and orange western sky], through which were seen long lines sweeping forward to the charge, and from whose depths came up, in a long frightful roll, the crash of small arms and the din of artillery, mingled with wild cheers, as the opposing ranks clashed one against the other....

The declining sun looked down upon a conflict... growing madder and more bloody as the shades of night drew near.

With intense but thoroughly suppressed excitement, Jackson moved to and fro, receiving dispatches, issuing orders... in the curt, brief accents which characterized him. He listened intently to the crash of musketry.... It was obvious that the Federal forces had not been repulsed, and toward dusk a courier galloped up and delivered a message from one of the generals that "the enemy did not give way."

Jackson's eyes glittered under his cap.... "Tell him if they stand at sunset to press them with the bayonet!"

... The musketry fire had been heavy before; it now became frightful. The... Confederate lines [along Lee's whole front] advanced, carrying all before them. In spite of the terrible fire from the triple line of Federal infantry on the ridge, and the incessant cannonade of the batteries in front and flank, they steadily swept on, and before this determined charge the Federal lines gave way....

The battle was over; and, posted in advance of his batteries... his figure clearly revealed by the fires which the shells had kindled [in the brush], Jackson, whose corps had decided the event, listened to the wild cheers of his men as they pressed the retreating enemy. . . .

The defeated Federals, leaving their dead but carrying as many of their wounded as they could, withdrew southward across the river, burning the bridges behind them, and joined their main body.

General McClellan spent the next day getting organized for his retreat, or "change of base," as he liked to call it. He knew that Lee would follow, and he fully expected to fight several battles along the way. A large part of the army's supplies had to be burned or otherwise destroyed for lack of room in the wagons. Much space had to be given to the wounded and the sick, who numbered in the thousands.

The great move southward toward Harrison's Landing on the James began on June 29, with the Confederates striking the rear of the column at Savage's Station that same day. They were repulsed, and the retreat continued.

Jackson's corps did not participate at Savage's Station, reaching the area only the next morning. This place had been selected for a meeting between Jackson and Lee. Robert Stiles, an artillery adjutant with Lee's original Richmond troops, who happened to be sitting against the trunk of a huge pine tree near the chosen spot, saw the meeting develop:

All of us had been longing for a sight of Jackson. It is impossible to exaggerate or even to convey an adequate idea of the excitement and furor concerning him . . . both in the army and among the people. . . .

Hearing the jingle of cavalry accoutrements . . . I looked up and saw a half-dozen mounted men, and riding considerably in advance a solitary horseman, whom I instantly recognized as the great wizard of the marvelous Valley Campaign which had so thrilled the army and the country.

Jackson and the little sorrel stopped in the middle of the road, probably not fifty feet off, while his staff halted perhaps a hundred and fifty yards in his rear. He sat stark and stiff in the saddle. Horse and rider appeared worn down to the lowest point of flesh consistent with effective service. His hair, skin, eyes, and clothes were all one neutral dust tint, and his badges of rank so dulled and tarnished as to be scarcely perceptible. The "mangy little cadet cap" was pulled so low in front that the visor cut the glint of his eyeballs.

A ghastly scene was spread across the road hard by. The [slain members of the] Seventeenth and Twenty-first Mississippi, of our brigade, had been . . . laid . . . in rows, with hands crossed upon the breast, but eyes wide-staring. A sickly summer rain had fallen in the night, and the faces . . . were bleached with more than death's pallor. . . . Men were passing through the silent lines, bending low, seeking in the distorted faces to identify their friends.

Jackson glanced a moment toward this scene. Not a muscle quivered as he resumed his steady gaze down the road toward Richmond. He was the ideal of concentration—imperturbable, resistless. I [got the] feeling that if he were not a very good man he would be a very bad one. By a ludicrous turn of the association of ideas, the old darkey minister's illustration of faith flashed through my brain:

"Bredren, ef de Lord tell me to jump through a stone wall, I's gwine to jump at it. Jumpin' at it 'longs to me; goin' through it 'longs to God."

The man before me would have jumped at anything the Lord told him to jump through.

A moment later and his gaze was rewarded. A magnificent staff approached from the direction of Richmond, and riding at its head, superbly mounted, a born king among men. . . . General Lee was one of the handsomest of men, especially on horseback, and . . . every detail of the dress and equipment of himself and horse was absolute perfection.

When he recognized Jackson he rode forward with a courier, his staff halting. As he gracefully dismounted, handing his bridle rein to his attendant, and advanced, drawing the gauntlet from his right hand, Jackson flung himself off his horse and advanced to meet Lee, Little Sorrel trotting back to the staff, where a courier secured him.

The two generals greeted each other warmly, but wasted no time upon the greeting. . . . Jackson began talking in a jerky, impetuous way, meanwhile drawing a diagram on the ground with the toe of his right boot . . . alternately looking up at Lee's face and down at his diagram. . . . At times I could hear their words, though they were uttered, for the most part, in the low tones of close and earnest conference.

As the two faced each other, except that the difference in

height was not great, the contrast between them could not have been more striking—in feature, figure, dress, voice, style, bearing, manner—everything, in short, that expressed the essential individuality of the two men. It was the Cavalier and the Puritan in intensest embodiment.

Still sitting against his tree trunk, Robert Stiles continued to watch with fascination as the conference ended and Jackson signaled for his horse:
    ... [He] vaulted awkwardly into the saddle and was off. Lee watched him a moment, the courier brought his horse, he mounted, and he and his staff rode away.

The plans made at this meeting did not work out. When Lee's columns caught up with McClellan a second time, about noon of that day, Jackson, who commanded the left wing of the attack, allowed himself to be stopped by a small, marshy stream and Federal cannon fire from the other side. As a result, Lee's right wing, fighting without support, was severely punished, and McClellan continued southward.
    Jackson's conduct at this battle (one given various names, including White Oak Swamp, Frayser's Farm, and Glendale) was ever afterward to be a matter of speculation. One of his officers said that the general was in a "peculiar mood" that afternoon. His friend and chief of staff Dr. Dabney ventures:
    This temporary eclipse of Jackson's genius was probably to be explained by physical causes. The labor of the previous days, the sleeplessness, the wear of gigantic cares, with the drenching of the comfortless night [Jackson had slept in the rain], had sunk the elasticity of his will and the quickness of his invention ... below their wonted tension.

McClellan next took up a position on Malvern Hill, only a few miles from his final destination. Establishing a strong defense line, he waited for Lee to attack.
    Jackson was up in ample time for this fight, which occurred on July 1. Explains General D. H. Hill:
    It was near noon when Jackson reached the immediate neighborhood of Malvern Hill. Some time was spent in reconnoitering, and in making tentative efforts with our few batteries to ascertain the strength and position of the enemy.
    I saw Jackson helping with his own hands to push [Captain

UNION GUN firing on Confederates at Malvern Hill.

James] Reilly's North Carolina battery farther forward. It was soon disabled, the woods around us being filled with shrieking and exploding shells.

I noticed an artilleryman seated comfortably behind a very large tree, and apparently feeling very secure. A moment later a shell passed through the huge tree and took off the man's head.

The Confederate attack was launched late in the afternoon, with Jackson's corps again on the left. Colonel John B. Gordon, one of Jackson's brigade commanders, witnessed an impressive example of the general's leadership:

I sat on my horse, facing him and receiving instructions from him, when Major General [W. H. C.] Whiting, himself an officer of high capacity, rode up in great haste and interrupted. . . .

With some agitation, Whiting said: "General Jackson, I find, sir, that I cannot accomplish what you have directed unless you send me some additional infantry and another battery." And he then proceeded to give the reasons why the order could not be executed with the forces at his disposal.

All this time, while Whiting explained and argued, Jackson sat on his horse like a stone statue. He looked neither to the right nor the left. He made no comment and asked no questions. But when Whiting had finished, Jackson turned his flashing eyes upon him and used these words, and only these: "I have told you what I wanted done, General Whiting." And, planting his spurs in his horse's sides, he dashed away at a furious speed to another part of the field.

Whiting gazed at Jackson's disappearing figure in amazement, if not in anger, and then rode back to his command. The result indicated the accuracy of Jackson's judgment... for Whiting did accomplish precisely what Jackson intended, and he did it with the force which Jackson had placed in his hands.

Gordon's observation of this incident, along with the knowledge that Jackson had done other things of a similar nature, prompted him to state:

... Jackson's wonderful power and success as a soldier ... was due not only to his keen and quick perception of the situation in which he found himself at each moment in the rapidly changing scenes as the battle progressed ... but notably to an implicit faith in his own judgment when once made up. He would formulate that judgment, risk his last man upon its correctness, and deliver the stunning blow—while others less gifted were hesitating and debating as to its wisdom and safety.

Jackson's uncommon abilities accomplished little at Malvern Hill. And the skills of Lee's other generals were equally ineffective. The Federals were too strongly posted. Moreover, the Confederate attack developed in a piecemeal way rather than as one heavy blow. In the end, with darkness covering the bloody field, the attackers withdrew, not only diminished in numbers but in a state of demoralization.

Jackson rode to the rear, had his servant prepare him a bed on the ground, and went to sleep. But many of the other officers stayed awake to confer and to worry. McClellan had been so successful against them

*that they feared he would launch a counterattack in the morning. A
party of Jackson's generals, deciding that their men would not be able to
stand against such an attack, went looking for Jackson to tell him.
Relates Jackson's medical director, Dr. Hunter McGuire:*

It was difficult to wake General Jackson, as he was exhausted
and very sound asleep. I tried it myself, and after many efforts,
partly succeeded. When he was made to understand what was
wanted he said: "McClellan and his army will be gone by day-
light," and went to sleep again.

*This incident, says Robert Stiles (the artillery adjutant who had wit-
nessed the meeting of Lee and Jackson),*

... illustrates two of the greatest and most distinguishing
traits and powers of Jackson as a general: he did not know what
demoralization meant, and he never failed to know just what
his adversary thought and felt and proposed to do. In the present instance, not only did all that Jackson said and implied
turn out to be true, that McClellan was thinking only of escape,
and never dreamed of viewing the Battle of Malvern Hill in any
other aspect, but in an incredibly short time our army had
recovered its tone and had come to take the same view of the
matter.

*The "Seven Days' Battles" ended with Malvern Hill, after which
McClellan took up his planned position under the guns of a Federal
fleet on the James. During the seven days of bloodshed, the Confederates
lost 20,000 men in killed, wounded, captured, and missing; the Federals lost 16,000.*

*Jackson's performance in this campaign had its highlights, but, gen-
erally speaking, wasn't up to his usual standards. Nonetheless McClellan had been driven from Richmond—thanks to Jackson's Valley Campaign, to Lee's leadership in the city's environs, and to the Federal
general's excessive caution.*

*As for McClellan's plans to launch a new campaign against
Richmond, they came to nothing. Lincoln could not provide him the
kind of reinforcements he said he needed. A month after Malvern Hill,
McClellan got orders from Washington to put his men aboard trans-
ports for shipment northward.*

ᴄ⁓VII.

Second Manassas

ᴄ⁓E̲ven while Lee was fighting McClellan's Army of the Potomac in the Richmond area, a new Federal army was forming to the north, between Richmond and Washington. Called the Army of Virginia, and numbering about 50,000 men, it was a gathering of the various units that had been operating individually around Washington and in the Shenandoah Valley.

The new army's commander was Major General John Pope, who had been summoned from the war's Western theater where, about three months earlier, he had made a reputation for himself by capturing Island Number Ten, in the Mississippi River at Kentucky's southwestern corner.

Pope claimed that in the West he had seen "only the backs" of the Confederates, and he spoke with great confidence of his plans against Lee. The Confederates named him "Pope the Braggart," and they laughed when it was reported he had informed Washington that his headquarters would be "in the saddle."

"It is strange," they said, "that a general should have his headquarters where his hindquarters ought to be."

Stonewall Jackson was told by an aide that Pope seemed to be demanding his attention. Said Jackson: "And, please God, he shall have it."

Pope's army began to loom in the north even before McClellan's army withdrew to its ships in the east. Actually, McClellan was a part of the new threat. He was expected to reinforce Pope by way of the Chesapeake Bay and the Potomac River. Such a junction of forces would give the Federals a powerful advantage, so Lee had to act quickly; he had to move against Pope before McClellan completed his evacuation of the Peninsula.

First to march northward to the new field was Stonewall Jackson. By this time many of his soldiers, after their months of busy campaigning, were in tatters, some of them even being barefoot. The South's resources were limited, and supplies were hard to come by. Considerable dependence was placed upon capturing vitally needed things from the Unionists.

Midday of August 9, 1862, found Jackson and his corps of some 24,000 men at Cedar Mountain, about halfway between Richmond and Washington (though west of the direct line). Pope's van was approaching this point.

Asked by his medical director, Dr. McGuire, whether he expected a battle that afternoon, Jackson replied: "Banks is in our front, and he is generally willing to fight." Then, murmuring into his beard, Jackson added, "And he generally gets whipped."

Banks came on furiously, as if determined to avenge his defeat in the Shenandoah Valley. Relates Confederate officer John Cooke:

So sudden and determined was this assault that the troops were almost surrounded before they knew it; and nothing remained for them but to fall back to a new position. The enemy gave them no time to reflect. They rushed forward with deafening yells, pouring a terrific fire into the wavering lines, and the day seemed lost. . . .

At this moment of disaster and impending ruin, Jackson appeared, amid the clouds of smoke, and his voice was heard rising above the thunder of the guns. The man, ordinarily so cool, silent, and deliberate, was now mastered by the genius of battle. . . . Galloping to the front, amid the heavy fire directed upon his disordered lines, now rapidly giving way—with his eyes flashing, his face flushed, his voice rising and ringing like a clarion on every ear, he rallied the confused troops. . . .

. . . they greeted him with resounding cheers. . . . The Federal advance was checked, the repulsed troops re-formed and led once more into action. . . . The bloody contest . . . terminated in the complete repulse of the Federal forces. . . .

As night descended upon the battlefield, a full moon rose. . . .

JOHN POPE.

The pallid beams fell on the upturned faces of the dead, the forms of the wounded, and upon countenances distorted in the last agony. Jackson had added another to the roll of his victories, and the weary troops who had won the day . . . lay down to sleep, the red battle flags fluttering above them in the dim moonlight.

A few days later Jackson was joined from the south by General Lee with James Longstreet and his corps, about 30,000 men. This gave the Confederates a numerical edge. What happened next is explained by an officer from Alabama, William C. Oates:

... Pope ... retreated.... And thus the braggart who had "never seen the rebels except their backs" was exhibiting to the rebels that interesting part of his own anatomy.

The Union general crossed to the north bank of the Rappahannock River, where he set up a defense line. He was now about fifty miles southwest of Washington. His position was a strong one, and he was expecting heavy reinforcements to arrive shortly, so he became quite willing to skirmish with Lee, who had deployed on the south side of the river.

Lee reacted by planning a very bold maneuver. He would divide his army, holding his front with Longstreet's corps while Jackson marched westward, swung around Pope's right flank, and came in about fifteen miles behind him, thus cutting him off from Washington. Lee's purpose was to confuse Pope and draw him northward from his strong position into a situation where he would be vulnerable. Lee intended to follow Jackson with Longstreet's corps in time to support him in a new confrontation.

Jackson first withdrew to the rear. In the words of Private John Casler:

As we passed through a small village we were ordered to leave our knapsacks in some vacant building.... We then knew what was up, the same as if Stonewall had told us. It simply meant a "forced march and a flank movement." We then turned our course westward up the Rappahannock, and, after marching some distance, crossed the river....

For the remainder of the first day, August 25, the columns headed northward. Says G. W. Nichols, a private from Georgia:

This march ... was terrible; it was very dry, the roads were very dusty, and the weather was desperately hot. We had a great many sunstrokes.... We were ... very short of provisions, because the supply trains could not catch up....

Adds one of the expedition's officers, Lieutenant John Chamberlayne:

... we marched ... across open fields, by strange country paths and comfortable homesteads, by a little town ... called Orleans, on and on, as if we would never cease—to Salem, on the Manassas Gap Railroad....

As the troops covered the terminal part of this first day's march, Jackson drew his horse to the side of the road to watch them pass. According to an unnamed member of his staff:

General Jackson ... looked with evident pleasure on the full and well-closed ranks; and when they commenced their usual cheering, he raised his hand to stop them, and all along the lines went the words, "Don't shout, boys; the Yankees will hear us."

The regiments passed by without music or noise; not even a loud-spoken word could be heard, nothing but the steady tramp of the men. As they passed, they raised their caps and waved them around their heads, and the enthusiastic love which beamed on every countenance showed how hard it was to suppress the usual greeting.

Those who saw General Jackson that evening as he sat on his horse, cap in hand, with the westering sun shining full on his firm kind face, could not say that he was without *pride*. He was full of it—his face all aglow with it; but it was for his men, not one iota for himself.

When they had all passed [with some of the latter regiments—those of the original Stonewall Brigade—cheering him wildly in spite of his request for silence], he turned and said: "Who could fail to win victory with those men?"

It was late at night when the troops settled down in the fields to sleep, and the stars were still bright when they were turned out to resume the march. On this day, August 26, they headed eastward. Relates Alabama's William Oates:

We passed through Bull Run Mountains at Thoroughfare Gap ... and reached the Alexandria Railroad at Bristoe Station was captured by some of the Fifteenth Alabama men, and between his army and Washington. We had marched nearly sixty miles in two days, and subsisted mainly on green corn and half-ripe apples hastily gathered from the fields and orchards we passed on the march. . . .

[At Bristoe Station] a number of Yankee officers were just sitting down to an excellent supper at the hotel when they were captured, and Jackson and his staff, very unwelcome and unexpected guests, took supper with them.

CONFEDERATE SOLDIER eating rations directly from the stalk.

That evening, Oates goes on to say, the Confederates placed obstructions on the railroad tracks and wrecked three trains that came puffing northward from Pope's lines, headed for Washington. The first two were thrown down an embankment, but the third was only lightly damaged.

"The engineer," Oates explains,
was captured by some of the Fifteenth Alabama men, and also two or three other prisoners, one of whom proved to be a civilian. . . . One of [the civilian's] legs was broken just above the ankle. He was laid upon the ground near a fire. He inquired who we were, and when informed he expressed a desire to see Stonewall Jackson.

I pointed out Jackson to him, who just then stood on the opposite side of the fire closely engaged in interrogating the engineer. He requested to be raised, which was done. He surveyed the great Confederate general in his dingy gray uniform, with his cap pulled down on his nose, for half a minute, and then in a tone of disappointment and disgust exclaimed, "O my God! Lay me down!"

Jeb Stuart and his horsemen were operating with Jackson at this time. That same night Stuart, along with some foot troops, proceeded five miles northeastward and occupied Manassas Junction, which held Pope's principal supply depot. Jackson's main body followed the next morning. After driving away a brigade of Federals who had approached from the Washington area, the men turned their attention to the supplies. Writes Lieutenant John Chamberlayne:

'Twas a curious sight to see our ragged and famished men helping themselves to every imaginable article of luxury or necessity, whether of clothing, food, or what not. For my part, I got a toothbrush, a box of candles, a quantity of lobster salad, a barrel of coffee, and other things. . . .

Our men . . . had brought no wagons, so we could carry little away of the riches before us. But the men could eat for one meal at least. . . . To see a starving man eating lobster salad and drinking Rhine wine, barefooted and in tatters, was curious.

Something else that was curious was noted by J. F. J. Caldwell, an officer from South Carolina: ". . . elegant . . . linen handkerchiefs were applied to noses hitherto blown with the thumb and forefinger. . . ."

Lieutenant Chamberlayne goes on to say that

The whole thing was incredible. . . . At nightfall, fire was set to the depot, storehouses, the loaded trains, several long empty trains, sutlers' houses [i.e., houses occupied by civilian merchants who did business with the soldiers], restaurants— everything.

The great fire that destroyed Pope's supplies could be seen in the night sky for many miles. A very unhappy observer was Pope himself. He had started his columns northward that day, his van driving Jackson's rear guard from Bristoe Station.

Pope decided that the chief purpose of Jackson's flank movement had been to destroy the supplies, and, figuring that Jackson would now try to escape, he hurried his troops along several roads in an effort to cut him off.

Jackson left Manassas Junction and took up a position just west of the old Manassas, or Bull Run, battlefield, where he had won his

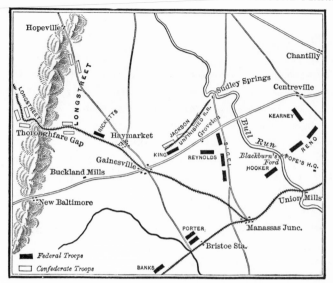

SECOND MANASSAS. Map shows situation on evening of August 28, as Jackson revealed his position to one of Pope's columns. Longstreet was beginning to make his way through Thoroughfare Gap. Pope, concentrating his scattered forces, attacked Jackson at the unfinished railroad the next morning. Jackson held until Longstreet arrived, and on August 30 Pope was driven eastward across Bull Run. Jackson struck Pope at Chantilly on September 1. Pope, having had enough, retreated to Washington.

famous nickname. On the evening of August 28 he deliberately revealed his position to Pope by attacking one of his columns as it was passing. This sharp but indecisive clash, which ended about nine o'clock, became known as the Battle of Groveton.

Pope hastened to order his other columns to converge in Jackson's front, feeling that he had the crafty Confederate where he wanted him. Pope's army, having been reinforced from the Peninsula, numbered about 70,000. Jackson, with less than 20,000, deployed for nearly two miles along the bed of an unfinished railroad, his lines facing eastward. Meanwhile Lee and Longstreet, marching northward by the same route Jackson had taken, were making their way through Thoroughfare Gap, about seven miles to the west.

The next morning Jackson readjusted his lines and awaited the Federal attack. His single advantage was that his men had the protection of the railroad bank. Skirmishing began early, the Federals advancing with bands playing and flags flying. From batteries in their rear, artillery shells came whistling over their heads to crash among the Confederates.

Heavier fighting began in the afternoon. "On came the Yankees," explains William Oates, of Jackson's Alabamans, "and the first attack we easily repulsed; but the next was more determined." Oates continues:

A major on horseback led his regiment up to the opposite side of the embankment and charged upon it, and Company A ... of the Fifteenth, killed the major and his horse on the embankment. Captain Feagin, when the firing ceased, rebuked the company for killing so brave a man and said they should have captured him.

General Jackson had ridden up in the woods in rear of the embankment and heard it. He said, "No, Captain, the men are right. Kill the brave ones; they lead on the others."

The Federals attacked again—and again. Cannons roared and muskets cracked; smoke rose in white wisps and in dark clouds; men shouted and horses neighed, with both species suffering heavy casualties. Through it all, Jackson rode along behind his lines, encouraging the men to stand fast and telling them that Longstreet was near at hand.

Lieutenant Chamberlayne says that after each attack the Federals fell back "shattered and shrieking." He goes on:

When the sun went down, their dead were heaped in front of the incomplete railway, and we sighed with relief, for Longstreet could be seen ... on our right. ... But the sun went down so slowly.

John Cooke sums up the situation:

What remained after the long and obstinate conflict—above the smoke, the dust, the blood—was this: Jackson had held his ground ... and Longstreet was there ... with his strong and veteran corps. Lee was by his side to take from his shoulders a portion of that burden of care and anxiety which would have crushed most men, and oppressed even the iron strength of Jackson. ...

As night came, thousands of campfires glowed in the opposing lines. Efforts were made from both sides to aid the great numbers of wounded

*who lay moaning and wailing in the darkness between. At last the fires
waned as the armies slept.*

*Dawn found General Lee preparing to renew the fight, while Pope
entertained the extraordinary idea that his foe was about to flee and
would have to be pursued.*

*The Confederates were outnumbered, but they had a peculiar advan-
tage. Because of the nature of the terrain—the lay of the hills and
woods—Pope could not see that Longstreet had come up in full force on
Jackson's right (that is, in front of Pope's left). Longstreet was on high
ground, his line angling forward from Jackson's, which gave him a
good view down Jackson's front. If Pope moved in and attacked Jackson
at close quarters, he would expose his left flank to Longstreet.*

*Pope had already made several mistakes in this campaign. He was
now about to make his greatest. In the words of William Owen, an
artillery adjutant with Longstreet's corps:*

At about 3 o'clock the enemy advanced . . . in heavy force, his
glittering lines of battle in magnificent array. Jackson's men
keep under cover of the railroad embankment until the enemy
come in close range, when all along their front suddenly comes
a crash of musketry. The enemy wavers and falls back.

Our men behind the railroad cut are running short of car-
tridges, and many run out and strip the dead and wounded of
their cartridge-boxes. A second and third line of the enemy, of
great strength, move up to support the first, and come forward
with apparently irresistible force. Jackson's men, having no
ammunition to spare, again await them until at close range, and
then pour their volleys into them with unerring aim; but the
enemy fights doggedly and well.

Many Confederates, getting out of ammunition, pick up
great stones and throw them into the faces of the foe with
deadly effect. The result of the fighting seems to tremble in the
balance, and Jackson sends for reinforcements, when the
enemy fortunately comes in range of the left flank of
Longstreet, who quickly orders four of the batteries of Col. S.
D. Lee's battalion to open upon him.

The effect is instantaneous; the heavy columns [of Federals],
until now holding their own or gradually pushing the hard-
fought and tired troops of Jackson, break and fall back in great
confusion. Their efforts to rally are unavailing; and, thus re-

A LINE of Jackson's men, their ammunition exhausted, fighting the advancing Federals with stones.

lieved of the pressure, Jackson's men leap out of the cut, and, pressing forward against the foe with wild shouts and yells, drive him in confusion and dismay. Then Longstreet, riding down his lines, gives the command to charge.... The men, eager and anxious for the fray, like bloodhounds unleashed, leap forward to help "Old Stonewall."

The counterattack took the shape of a great semicircle, with Jackson on the left and Longstreet on the right. A richly setting sun behind the Confederates brightened their red flags, bronzed their bayonets, and cast long shadows before them. The Federals made efforts to turn and stand, their cannons and muskets sometimes crashing as loudly as those of their foes. But, yard by yard, they were driven eastward across the familiar terrain of First Manassas, past the grave and the ruined home of the Widow Henry, toward the Stone Bridge over Bull Run. Says General Longstreet:

Farther and still farther back we pressed them, until at 10

o'clock at night we had the field. Pope was across Bull Run, and the victorious Confederates lay down on the battleground to sleep, while all around were strewn thousands—friend and foe—sleeping the last sleep together.

The work of Jackson's fatigued and battered corps was still not over. Pope drew up at Centreville, twenty miles west of Washington, and on September 1 General Lee sent Jackson around to the north on another flank attack. Pope dispatched a part of his army to meet it.

With the Battle of Chantilly about to begin, John Cooke got a memorable glimpse of Jackson:

The Federal forces were then in motion from Centreville, and the skirmishers on the right were already engaged. The rifles were cracking and the balls beginning to fly, but Jackson . . . was asleep. Seated at the foot of a tree, with his chin upon his breast, his cap drawn over his eyes, and his hands crossed on his breast, as though he had fallen asleep while praying, he slept as peacefully as a child. . . .

He was soon aroused; duty called him, and, mounting his horse, he took the head of his column and advanced to deliver battle on another field.

The troops that Jackson went up against were fresh ones, reinforcements from McClellan's Army of the Potomac, just back from the Peninsula. Jackson's medical director, Dr. McGuire, says that the battle was fought "during a heavy thunderstorm, when the voice of the artillery of heaven could scarcely be told from that of the army." McGuire goes on:

. . . an aide came up [to Jackson] with a message from A. P. Hill that his ammunition was wet, and that he asked leave to retire.

"Give my compliments to General Hill, and tell him that the Yankee ammunition is as wet as his; to stay where he is."

There was always danger and blood when he began his terse sentences with "Give my compliments."

Jackson's attack was held off, but General Pope decided that his Army of Virginia would be safer behind the defenses of Washington, where he promptly took it. This ended the campaign of Second Manassas. Casualties had come to about 15,000 for the Federals (killed, wounded, captured, and missing), and about 10,000 for the Confederates.

"Pope the Braggart," with a large and splendid army, had, like McClellan, been bested by an army that was modestly numbered, hungry, ragged, and ill equipped—an army with but two assets: able leadership and a tremendous fighting spirit.

Again in the words of Confederate officer John Cooke:

Pope—like Banks, Frémont, Shields, and Milroy—had passed away, his lurid star obscured by the clouds of disaster and defeat. The star of Jackson mounted toward the zenith—it was the star of victory.

Traveling with the Southern army at this time was Francis Lawley, special correspondent of the London Times, *who wrote that Jackson was beginning to command "universal wonder and admiration." Lawley says that like Hannibal (the Carthaginian general of ancient times) Jackson was content to live among his men without distinction, little caring that he often went unrecognized. The correspondent makes another comparison:*

... they who have seen and heard him uplift his voice in prayer, and then have witnessed his vigor and prompt energy in the strife, say that once again Cromwell [i.e., Oliver Cromwell, 1599–1658, England's Puritan general and statesman] is walking the earth and leading his trusting and enraptured hosts to assured victory.

Lawley ventures the opinion that "the interest excited by this strange man is as curious as it is unprecedented," and adds:

A classmate of McClellan at West Point, and there considered slow and heavy, unfavorably known in Washington as a hypochondriac and *malade imaginaire* [imaginary invalid], he has exhibited for the last ten months qualities which were little supposed to reside in his rugged and unsoldierlike frame, but which will hand his name down for many a generation in the company of those great captains whom men will not willingly let die.

～VIII.

Sharpsburg

～*T*he outcome of the Second Manassas Campaign filled the South with elation and the North with alarm. As expressed by Edward A. Pollard, editor of the Richmond Examiner:

Now the war was transferred from the gates of Richmond to those of Washington. . . . A terrible situation was before [the North's] eyes. The Confederates . . . would certainly attempt a new adventure; and so greatly had they risen in the opinion of their enemies that no project was thought too extravagant, or enterprise too daring, for the troops of Lee and Jackson.

These generals had no intention of making a direct assault upon Washington; they hadn't the strength for this. What they planned was a march northward, on a course about twenty-five miles west of the capital, into the Union-held state of Maryland. This state had many Southern sympathizers, and the Confederates believed an invasion would secure them not only much-needed supplies but thousands of recruits.

The army might be strengthened enough to threaten Washington or to strike farther northward into Union territory. The North might be sufficiently alarmed to end the war on Southern terms—especially if a great battle could be won on Northern soil.

If a successful invasion did not end the war, it might well prompt England and France, who were sympathetic to the Confederate cause, to grant the South recognition as an independent nation and to intervene in the war on her behalf. England was already dispatching military goods that got through to the Confederates in spite of a Union naval blockade of their ports.

On September 3, 1862, only two days after the Battle of Chantilly, Lee started his columns northward. His opponent in this campaign was to be George B. McClellan, whom he had beaten on the Peninsula. As Pope fell from grace, McClellan was given the task of merging the Virginia armies into a revitalized Army of the Potomac. Now he put his troops on a course parallel to Lee, some miles to the east, his purpose to cover Washington and Baltimore.

Stonewall Jackson led the invasion. One of Jackson's first acts was to arrest division commander A. P. Hill for allowing his men to straggle. Hill would soon be reinstated to his command, but he and Jackson were to remain at odds. As for the problem of straggling, which became serious on this march, Jackson ordered that men who left the ranks without good reason were to be shot.

Relates Henry Kyd Douglas, of Stonewall's staff:

On the 5th of September Jackson crossed the Potomac at White's Ford, a few miles beyond Leesburg. The passage of the river by the troops marching in fours, well closed up—the laughing, shouting, and singing, as a brass band in front played "Maryland, My Maryland," was a memorable experience ... but we were not long in finding out that if General Lee had hopes that the decimated regiments of his army would be filled by the sons of Maryland he was doomed to a speedy and unqualified disappointment.

However, before we had been in Maryland many hours, one enthusiastic citizen presented Jackson with a gigantic gray mare. She was a little heavy and awkward for a war horse, but as the general's Little Sorrel had a few days before been temporarily stolen, the present was a timely one. . . .

Yet ... the next morning when he mounted his new steed and touched her with his spur the ... undisciplined beast reared straight into the air, and ... threw herself backward, horse and rider rolling upon the ground. The general was stunned and severely bruised, and lay upon the ground for some time before he could be removed. He was then placed in an ambulance, where he rode during the day's march. . . .

Early that day the army went into camp near Frederick, and

JACKSON'S CORPS wading the Potomac River at White's Ford.

Generals Lee, Longstreet, Jackson, and for a time Jeb Stuart had their headquarters near one another in Best's Grove. Hither in crowds came the good people of Frederick, especially the ladies, as to a fair.

General Jackson, still suffering from his hurt, kept to his tent, busying himself with maps and official papers, and declined to see visitors. Once, however, when he had been called to General Lee's tent, two young girls waylaid him, paralyzed him with smiles and embraces and questions, and then jumped into their carriage and drove off rapidly, leaving him there, cap in hand, bowing, blushing, and speechless. But once safe in his tent he was seen no more that day.

The next evening, Sunday, he went into Frederick . . . to attend church. . . . As usual he fell asleep, but this time more soundly than was his wont. His head sunk upon his breast, his cap dropped from his hands to the floor; the prayers of the congregation did not disturb him, and only the choir and the deep-toned organ awakened him.

... the minister was credited with much loyalty and courage because he had prayed for the President of the United States in the very presence of Stonewall Jackson. Well, the general didn't hear the prayer. . . .

The Federal army under McClellan was at this time some miles south-east of Frederick. McClellan was proceeding cautiously, as usual—this time with good reason, for he was uncertain of Lee's intentions. Lee's army numbered about 55,000 men. McClellan's strength was building toward 90,000; but information he got from his cavalry scouts convinced him he was outnumbered, that Lee had 110,000—twice his actual number.

Lee decided to head westward, and the army marched through Frederick on September 10. Staff officer Douglas, who rode at Jackson's side, sets something straight:

Just a few words here in regard to Mr. [John Greenleaf] Whittier's touching poem, "Barbara Frietchie." An old woman by that . . . name did live in Frederick . . . but she never saw General Jackson, and General Jackson never saw Barbara Frietchie. I was with him every minute of the time he was in that city. . . . Mr. Whittier must have been misinformed as to the incident.

[Whittier's poem claims that Jackson ordered his men to shoot down the old woman's Union flagstaff; then, shamed by the courage she showed in grabbing the falling banner and waving it by hand, allowed her to fly it unmolested.]

On the march that day . . . we entered each village . . . before the inhabitants knew of our coming. In Middletown two very pretty girls, with ribbons of red, white, and blue floating from their hair, and small Union flags in their hands, rushed out of a house as we passed, came to the curbstone, and with much laughter waved their flags defiantly in the face of the general.

He bowed and raised his hat, and, turning with his quiet smile to his staff, said: "We evidently have no friends in this town."

And that is about the way he would have treated Barbara Frietchie!

On this westward march, Lee's columns were dispersed. He planned to reunite them at Hagerstown, beyond Maryland's South Mountain.

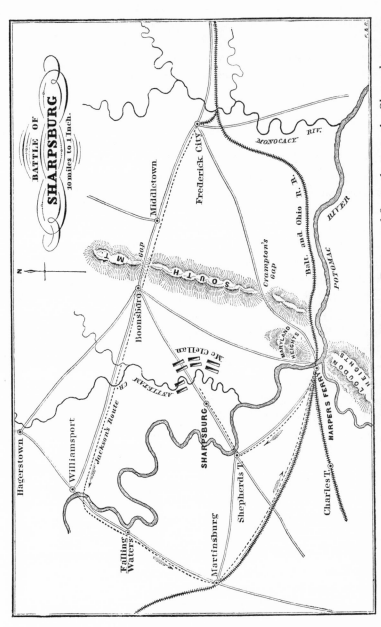

MAP SHOWS JACKSON'S ROUTE from Frederick to Harpers Ferry, and from there to the Sharpsburg, or Antietam, battlefield. Confederate lines are not shown. They faced those of McClellan on a north-south line through Sharpsburg.

First, Jackson was to take Harpers Ferry, to the southwest. The northern gateway to the Shenandoah Valley had to be opened so that Lee could use the Valley as his avenue of communications with the South.

Passing over South Mountain at Turner's Gap, Jackson marched toward Harpers Ferry by the roundabout way of Williamsport and Martinsburg. Two columns moving by more direct routes were to meet him at the objective.

The country just short of Martinsburg was the scene of one of Jackson's night camps. Here, according to Douglas, the general did something unusual:

Fatigued by the day's march, Jackson was persuaded by his host of the night [a rural homeowner] to drink a whisky toddy—the only glass of spirits I ever saw him take. While mixing it leisurely, he remarked that he believed he liked the taste of whisky and brandy more than any soldier in the army; that they were more palatable to him than the most fragrant coffee, and for that reason, with others, he rarely tasted them.

The next morning the Confederates entered Martinsburg. Here the general was welcomed with great enthusiasm. . . . The crowd, chiefly ladies . . . embarrassed the general with every possible outburst of affection, to which he could only reply, "Thank you, you're very kind."

He gave them his autograph in books and on scraps of paper, cut a button from his coat for a little girl, and then submitted patiently to an attack by the others, who soon stripped the coat of nearly all the remaining buttons. But when they looked beseechingly at his hair, which was thin, he drew the line there, and managed to close the interview.

Jackson's column approached Harpers Ferry from the west, the other two columns from the east. Jackson was in overall command. The town surrendered, after only minor resistance, on September 15. Writes Confederate officer J. F. J. Caldwell:

We entered and took possession. The captures consisted of eleven thousand prisoners, twelve thousand stand of arms, seventy pieces of artillery, the horses and harness thereto attached, a large number of wagons, and an immense supply of stores. . . . We fared sumptuously. In addition to meat, crackers, sugar, coffee, shoes, blankets, underclothing, etc., many of us captured horses roaming at large, on whom to transport our plunder. . . .

The ragged, forlorn appearance of our men excited the combined merriment and admiration of our prisoners. . . . But Jackson was the great theme of conversation. The Federals seemed never weary of extolling his genius and inquiring for particulars of his history. They were extremely anxious to see him, and made many of us promise to show him to them if he should pass among us that day.

He came up from the river side late in the afternoon. The intelligence spread like electricity. Almost the whole mass of prisoners broke over us, rushed to the road, threw up their hats, cheered, roared, bellowed, as even Jackson's own troops had scarcely ever done. We, of course, joined in with them. The

A GLIMPSE
of Jackson.

general gave a stiff acknowledgment of the compliment...
drove spurs into his horse, and went clattering down the hill,
away from the noise.

*During Jackson's investment of Harpers Ferry, General Lee had run
into serious trouble some miles to the north. Shortly after the Confederate columns had marched westward from Frederick and passed over
South Mountain, McClellan's Federals had reached Frederick from the
east. On an abandoned Confederate campground, one of McClellan's
men found a copy of the order in which Lee explained his campaign
plans to his top generals. How this vital paper came to be lost was never
to be explained.*

*On the morning of September 14, McClellan moved westward to the
South Mountain passes. The Confederates opposed him there, and a day
of bitter fighting resulted. McClellan, with his superior numbers, was
the victor, but Lee gained enough time to begin setting up a defense line
to the west, at Sharpsburg. Facing eastward, the line overlooked the
shallow valley of Antietam Creek.*

*Jackson was desperately needed on this line. Leaving A. P. Hill's
division to complete the surrender arrangements at Harpers Ferry, he
hurried to Sharpsburg. Lee placed him on the left. Longstreet was on the
right.*

*General McClellan established his line on the slopes east of the Anti-
etam Creek on September 15 and 16, a preliminary skirmish occurring
on the latter day. By dawn of the seventeenth, Lee, with a scant 40,000
men, was facing some 80,000 Federals poised for a general attack.*

*Relates Confederate officer John B. Gordon, whose position in the
center of Lee's line gave him a view of the entire field:*

As these vast American armies, the one clad in blue and the
other in gray, stood contemplating each other from the adja-
cent hills, flaunting their defiant banners, they presented an
array of martial splendor that was not equalled, perhaps, on
any other field. It was in marked contrast with other battle-
grounds.

... there were no breastworks, no abatis, no intervening
woodlands, nor abrupt hills, nor hiding places, nor impassable
streams. The space over which the assaulting columns were to
march ... consisted of smooth and gentle undulations and a
narrow valley covered with green grass and growing corn....

On the elevated points [across] the narrow valley the Union

batteries were rolled into position, and the Confederate heavy
guns unlimbered to answer them. For one or more seconds,
and before the first sounds reached us, we saw the great vol-
umes of white smoke rolling from the mouths of McClellan's
artillery. The next second brought the roar of the heavy discharges and the loud explosions of hostile shells in the midst of
our lines, inaugurating the great battle.

The Confederate batteries promptly responded; and while
the artillery of both armies thundered, McClellan's compact
columns of infantry fell upon the left of Lee's lines [where
Jackson commanded] with the crushing weight of a landslide.

The Confederate battle line was too weak to stand the
momentum of such a charge. Pressed back [toward the site of a
small Dunkard church], but neither hopelessly broken nor dis-
mayed, the Southern troops . . . reformed their lines, and with a
shout as piercing as the blast of a thousand bugles, rushed in

CASUALTIES of Sharpsburg. Dunkard church in background.

counter-charge upon the exulting Federals, hurled them back in confusion, and recovered all the ground that had been lost.

Again and again, hour after hour, by charges and counter-charges, this portion of the field was lost and recovered, until the green corn that grew upon it looked as if it had been struck by a storm of bloody hail. . . . There was [at length] an ominous lull. . . . From sheer exhaustion, both sides, like battered and bleeding athletes, seemed willing to rest.

Says the director of Jackson's medical corps, Dr. McGuire:
About 1 o'clock . . . I rode forward to see the General. I found him a little to the left of the Dunkard Church. . . . I had my saddle pockets filled with peaches to take to him—knowing how much he enjoyed fruit—and was eating a peach when I approached him. The first thing he asked me was if I had any more. I told him yes, that I had brought him some. After he got them he began to eat them ravenously, so much so that he apologized and told me he had had nothing to eat that day. . . .

He was perfectly cool and quiet, although he had withstood three separate attacks of vastly superior numbers. He thought the enemy had done their worst. . . .

Before returning to my post I rode forward with him to see the old Stonewall Division. They had been reduced to a very small body of men and were commanded by Col. [A. J.] Grigsby. . . . While talking to Grigsby, I saw off at a distance in a field men lying down, and supposed it was a line of battle.

I asked Colonel Grigsby why he did not move that line of battle [back] to make it conform to his own, when he said, "Those men . . . are all dead. . . . They are Georgia soldiers."

As Jackson believed, McClellan had no further plans to test the Confederate left. By Lee's orders, Jackson looked for a way to launch a counterstroke, but none could be found.

The second round of Union attacks hit Lee's center—and the "Bloody Lane" was added to the war's annals. Here the dead were spread in twisted masses. And here the Confederate line was broken. Had McClellan followed through and sent in his reserves, Lee might well have been dealt a smashing defeat. But as usual McClellan believed that it was Lee, not he, who had the advantage of numbers.

The final fighting of the day occurred on Lee's right, with Union

General Ambrose Burnside attacking across the Antietam Creek and advancing on Sharpsburg. This section of the line was saved by the timely arrival of A. P. Hill from Harpers Ferry. Burnside was driven back to the creek.

When the shooting ended at sunset, the opposing lines were in about the same positions they had held at dawn. This was to become known as "the bloodiest day of the war." Lee lost about 10,000 men, McClellan about 12,000.

Little happened the following day. Lee held his ground, and McClellan, though strongly reinforced, was "stared down." But Lee knew that his invasion of the North had failed. During the night of September 18–19, the Confederates made an orderly retreat, fording the Potomac at nearby Shepherdstown and entering the northern end of the Shenandoah Valley. Jackson brought up the rear. According to Private G. W. Nichols:

A part of McClellan's forces followed the retreating Confederates [across the river]. Jackson . . . made a dash on them and drove them panic-stricken back. Some of the Union army fell off the bluff, fifty or sixty feet, into the river and were killed.

Private Nichols elaborates on this account with an anecdote. He begins by explaining that the Confederates had been obliged to leave many of their sick and wounded on the Sharpsburg battlefield, a few medical aides remaining with them:

When the Union army was passing through the . . . battlefield [to begin its pursuit], one little Dutchman went by the hospital tents where our hospital nurse, [William] Alderman, was cooking for the sick and wounded. . . . Alderman . . . asked him where he was going.

The Dutchman replied, "We dosh be going to hunt Shockson."

Alderman said the little Dutchman was gone about three hours and returned wet all over and his hat and gun gone. He had been churning the Potomac River trying to get back. . . . Alderman . . . asked him if he found Jackson.

The Dutchman replied, "Vel, yas, and he dosh give us *hell* dish day!"

~IX.

Fredericksburg

~ *Though President Lincoln urged General McClellan to persist in his efforts against the retreating Confederates, McClellan chose to settle down north of the Potomac and reorganize and resupply his army. Apparently unaware that he still outnumbered Lee more than 2 to 1, he told Lincoln that he had to have more men before he could press into Virginia.*

McClellan's attitude, of course, worked to Lee's advantage. Much more than McClellan, Lee needed time to go into camp and reorganize, resupply, and reinforce his army. He ended his retreat at once, still at the Valley's northern end. Thus it was, says Confederate officer John Cooke, that Jackson's troops

... passed the beautiful month of October [1862] in ... that region which their leader had already made so famous. There ... the army rested and recovered its strength and spirits. ... Jackson had his headquarters near Bunker's Hill and was often seen moving to and fro among his troops on his old sorrel horse. ...

The private soldiers took great pride in the moments when Jackson stopped to pass a few words with them. One day a man went about his camp boasting that the general had paid him very special attention that morning.

Asked what Jackson said, the private replied: "He asked me what I

was doing in that orchard over yonder; said he expected his men to have
more respect for people's property—and he told me to march right out."
    Again in the words of John Cooke:

[I] scanned curiously . . . the appearance of the soldier with
whose praises the whole land was ringing. He wore his dingy
old uniform and cavalry boots, but the ladies of Martinsburg
had robbed him not only of his buttons but his old cap. [Actu-
ally, it seems that the cap was claimed as a souvenir by one of
Jackson's own men, Major Jed Hotchkiss.]

The individual in the tall black hat, with the brim turned
down Quaker-wise all round, scarcely seemed to be the veritable Stonewall Jackson. But greater changes still were to ensue in
his personal appearance.

Cavalry leader Jeb Stuart, who liked and admired Jackson, had a
Richmond tailor make him a new coat. It was delivered to Jackson's
camp by Major Heros von Borcke, a Prussian officer serving as Stuart's
chief of staff. Von Borcke relates that he found Jackson in his headquar-
ters tent:

. . . I produced General Stuart's present, in all its magnifi-
cence of gilt buttons and sheeny facings and gold lace, and I
was heartily amused at the modest confusion with which the
hero of many battles regarded the fine uniform from many
points of view, scarcely daring to touch it, and at the quiet way
in which, at last, he folded it up carefully and deposited it in his
portmanteau, saying to me:

"Give Stuart my best thanks, my dear Major. The coat is
much too handsome for me, but I shall take the best care of it,
and shall prize it highly as a souvenir. And now let us have some
dinner."

But I protested energetically against this summary disposi-
tion of the matter of the coat, deeming my mission, indeed, but
half executed, and remarked that Stuart would certainly ask me
how the uniform fitted its owner, and that I should, therefore,
take it as a personal favour if he would put it on.

To this he readily assented with a smile, and, having donned
the garment, he escorted me outside the tent to the table where
dinner had been served in the open air. The whole of the staff
were in a perfect ecstacy at their chief's brilliant appearance. . . .

Meanwhile, the rumour of the change ran like electricity

through the neighbouring camps, and the soldiers came running by hundreds to the spot, desirous of seeing their beloved Stonewall in his new attire. . . .

Jackson was promoted to lieutenant general on October 11. He found no particular pleasure in this, writing his wife that the only really important job in the world was that of the minister who preached "the Gospel of the Prince of Peace."

At the end of October the Union's General McClellan finally got started southward from Maryland. It took him a week just to get his army across the Potomac into Virginia. By this time President Lincoln had lost all patience with the timid general. On November 7, during a snowstorm, an agent from Washington arrived at McClellan's camp near Warrenton and told him he was through. His job went to one of his corps commanders, General Ambrose Burnside.

Burnside accepted the high office with misgivings, feeling that his talents were not up to it. But he soon made plans to press the war, deciding to march southward to Fredericksburg as the first step in a new campaign against Richmond. General Lee divined his intentions and moved to intercept him, ordering Longstreet southeast toward Fredericksburg. Similar orders soon reached Jackson.

JACKSON as a lieutenant general.

An incident of Stonewall's march is described by an unnamed staff officer who was with him:

... General Jackson, with his staff, riding some two or three miles in front of his army ... met a very old woman looking for her grandson, who was somewhere in the army. As we passed, she hailed the General, saying, "Are you Mr. Jackson?" He told her he was, and asked what she wanted.

"I want to see my grandson, George Martin. He belongs to your company. I've brought him these clothes and victuals."

The General asked her what regiment her grandson was in, but she could not tell.... All she could tell was that he was "in Mr. Jackson's company." In her disappointment, she cried:

"Why, Mr. Jackson, don't you know little George Martin— George Augustus Martin? He's been with you in all your battles. And they say," she added, with tears streaming down her furrowed cheeks, "that he fit as hard as the best of them."

At this point some of the younger members of the staff laughed. The General turned around quickly with his brow contracted, his lips compressed, and his eyes flashing with anger....

Dismounting from his horse and approaching the old woman, he, in the kindest manner and simplest words, explained why he did not know her grandson; but gave her such simple and repeated directions as would enable her to find him.

While Jackson was on his way to Fredericksburg, he became the father of a daughter. Receiving the news from Mary Anna, he wrote back: "Oh! How thankful I am to our kind Heavenly father.... I cannot tell you ... how much I wish I could be with you and see my two darlings."

Early December found Burnside's Army of the Potomac in full force on the northeast side of the Rappahannock River at Fredericksburg. Longstreet's corps of Lee's Army of Northern Virginia was on the southwest side. The armies were from a mile to two miles apart, both overlooking the river valley from commanding heights. The town was on the Confederate bank, in front of the heights held by Longstreet. Lee had decided to await Burnside's attack.

On December 11 the Federals laid pontoon bridges and captured the town, bombarding it heavily in the process. The next day Jackson deployed his corps along wooded heights on Longstreet's right, the position overlooking a broad expanse of fields leading down to the river south-

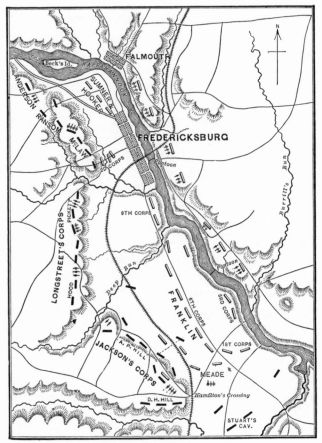

THE BATTLE of Fredericksburg.

east of the town. Jackson had the support of Jeb Stuart and his horse
artillery.

Even while Jackson deployed, the Federals of General William B.
Franklin's corps could be seen in front, crossing the river on pontoon
bridges and spreading out along the bank.

By the morning of December 13, Burnside was ready to attack both
Longstreet and Jackson. The Federal commander had about 120,000
men at his call, while Lee had less than 80,000.

A frosty fog covered the hills, the fields, and the town until ten o'clock,
when the day turned sunny and blue. General Longstreet was at this
time with Lee on a hill near the center of the long defense line, and while
he waited for the Federals to stream out of the town and attack his wing,
he watched a show that had begun to his right, on the plain in front of
Jackson:

Franklin's 40,000 men, reinforced by two divisions of [General Joseph] Hooker's grand division, were in front of Jackson's 30,000. The flags of the Federals fluttered gayly, the polished arms shone brightly in the sunlight, and the beautiful uniforms of the buoyant troops gave to the scene the air of a holiday occasion. . . .

I could see almost every soldier Franklin had, and a splendid array it was. . . . Jackson's ragged infantry and . . . Stuart's battered cavalry . . . [were] a striking contrast to the handsomely equipped troops of the Federals.

There was one startling exception among the poorly dressed Confederates—Stonewall Jackson. Explains James Power Smith, an aide who rode along the lines with Jackson just before the battle began:
He wore the new and handsome coat, the present of . . . Stuart, and a new cap sent him by his wife, with a wide braid of gilt about it. . . . He had a new officer's saber and spurs, sent him by Colonel [Robert] White of the cavalry. Altogether he looked so very spick and span that the boys could scarcely believe their eyes, so unlike was he to the battered, sunburnt "Old Jack" of the Valley.

Some of the troops cheered their approval of Jackson's transformation. Others shook their heads and joked wryly about it, claiming to be afraid that Jackson would be so careful to keep from soiling his new clothes that he wouldn't get down to work.
The work was about to begin, the Federals launching their attack with an artillery bombardment. At this moment Major Heros von Borcke, of Stuart's staff, arrived to consult with Jackson:
I found Old Stonewall standing at ease upon his hill, unmoved in the midst of the terrible fire, narrowly observing the movements of the enemy through his field-glass. . . .

On they came, in beautiful order, as if on parade, a moving forest of steel, their bayonets glistening. . . . On they came . . . [over] the wintry landscape, while their artillery beyond the river continued the cannonade with unabated fury over their heads, and gave a background of white fleecy smoke, like midsummer clouds, to the animated picture.

I could not rid myself of a feeling of depression and anxiety as I saw this innumerable host steadily moving upon our lines, which were hidden by the woods, where our artillery main-

A PART of Jackson's line during the Battle of Fredericksburg. Men in foreground await orders as gun at upper left fires upon advancing Federals.

tained as yet a perfect silence, General Lee having given orders that our guns should not open fire until the Yankees had come within easy canister range.

Upon my mentioning this feeling to Jackson, the old chief answered me in his characteristic way: "Major, my men have sometimes failed to *take* a position, but to *defend* one, never. . . ."

This record was kept intact, though the struggle was a fierce one. First, young Captain John Pelham, of Stuart's horse artillery, whose guns were stationed forward of Jackson's right flank, made a name for himself by delaying the entire Federal advance for half an hour.

Recovering, the blue lines came on, their artillery fire shrieking over their heads but finding few targets. As the Federals neared the wooded heights, Jackson's concealed batteries opened with a resounding crash and sent them reeling. A long artillery duel followed, with the infantry of both sides hugging the trembling ground.

Advancing again, the Federals hit a weak spot in the line and made a serious penetration. Jackson, showing no trace of alarm, ordered up his reserves. These men charged through the woods with the rebel yell, and the bluecoats were driven back at the point of the bayonet.

The countercharge continued until it collided with sixteen Federal guns pouring forth canister. Heavy losses ensued, the survivors falling back in disorder. But the Federals themselves had been badly hurt; they did not pursue.

Meanwhile, the Federal units in front of Longstreet had come out of Fredericksburg and attacked his position on Marye's Heights. A long day of the most courageous advances brought the bluecoats nothing but disaster. Artillery shells rained down on them, and they made no progress against the key to the position, a long stone wall from behind which came volley after volley of murderous musket fire.

Major von Borcke, of Jackson's lines, says of the field as a whole:

About seven o'clock the battle ceased for the day; only random cannon shots were still interchanged, the flight of the shells distinctly marked in flaming curves across the dark firmament, and the shadows of evening fell upon a battlefield ... where thousands of mutilated and dying men lay in hopeless anguish, writhing in their wounds, and pitilessly exposed to the sharp frosty air of the winter's night.

At a cost of some 5,000 casualties, Jackson and Longstreet had inflicted well over 12,000. As Jackson returned to his camp in the company of Dr. McGuire, he said wearily, "How horrible is war!" The doctor pointed out that in this war the Federals were the aggressors, that they had invaded the South. He closed with the question, "What can we do?" Jackson's demeanor changed, his blood rising. "Do?" he said sharply. "Why, shoot them!"

The scene at headquarters that evening presented a strong contrast to that on the battlefield. In the words of Jackson's aide, James Smith:

A party of gentlemen had arrived from Richmond: Hon. Alexander Boteler and others, and with them Mr. Volke, a sculptor. Mr. Boteler had brought a large bucket of oysters, and the cook made us a supper of oysters and our ordinary camp fare that was greatly enjoyed.

After the supper, the general was requested to allow Mr. Volke to make some sketches of him. The party gathered in the general's tent, where the artist went to work with his pencils. Going out of the tent for a few minutes, on my return I found the gentlemen all in broad smiles, and the general himself, sitting erect on his camp stool, quite sound asleep.

It wasn't known on the night of December 13 that the battle was over. Union General Burnside wanted to renew the attack the next day, but his subordinates convinced him this would be a mistake. Therefore the fourteenth, a Sunday, saw only some cannon fire and some musket exchanges among the men of the picket lines (and Jackson had ample time for his devotionals).

When night fell, many of the more threadbare Confederates crept out on the battlefield and robbed the Federal dead of their clothing. The next day a truce was arranged so that the wounded still on the field could be cared for.

That night, says Confederate officer John Cooke,

... the Federal army commenced recrossing the river. By Tuesday morning the forces had disappeared from the south bank [leaving behind a great scattering of equipment and many unburied dead] ... and General Burnside's was another name added to the list of Federal generals who had suffered defeat at the hands of Lee and Jackson.

≈ X. ∞

Chancellorsville

⌒J anuary, 1863, found the opposing armies in winter quarters at Fredericksburg, the Federals on the ground they had occupied before the battle and the Confederates stretched out along the bank they had defended so well.

Stonewall Jackson, having established his headquarters in a small house on a country estate some miles southeastward along the river, spent the cold months completing the official reports of his various battles and preparing his corps for new fighting in the spring.

An incident of the winter is related by Jackson's aide, James Smith:

One day there came a note from Lee asking Jackson to come to see him at his convenience. In the evening Jackson said he would ride up there the next morning and directed me to be ready to accompany him. When the early morning came, the country lay under a heavy fall of snow and the cold was severe, with the snow still falling. I turned over in my blanket and went to sleep again, thinking that the general would not go. But an orderly awoke me, saying that the general was ready to mount and waiting for me.

I was soon in the saddle by his side, without my breakfast, and a worse ride than that one, in the face of the storm for twelve or fourteen miles, I never had. General Lee was surprised and quite indignant that General Jackson had come. Walking out into the snow without his hat, he reproached

Jackson, saying, "You know I did not wish you to come in such a storm. It was a matter of little importance. I am so sorry that you have had this ride."

Jackson blushed and smiled and said: "I received your note, General Lee!"

In mid-March, Jackson moved back up the river, establishing his head-quarters in a tent on the old battleground. On April 20, Mary Anna Jackson arrived by train from North Carolina, bringing with her five-month-old Julia Jackson, whom the general had never seen. Says Mary Anna:

When he entered the coach to receive us, his rubber overcoat was dripping from the rain which was falling, but his face was all sunshine and gladness; and . . . it was a picture, indeed, to see his look of perfect delight and admiration as his eyes fell upon that baby!

Mary Anna and Julia were lodged at a house less than a mile from Jackson's headquarters, and he spent as much time with them as his duties permitted. The baby, of course, was the center of attention. Again in Mary Anna's words:

. . . he rarely had her out of his arms, walking her and amusing her in every way that he could think of—sometimes holding her up before a mirror and saying, admiringly, "Now, Miss Jackson, look at yourself!" Then he would turn ... and say: "Isn't she a *little gem?*"

. . . When she slept ... he would often kneel over her cradle and gaze upon her little face with the most rapt admiration, and he said he felt almost as if she were an angel. . . .

Jackson's wife and daughter were with him for nine days. They left as the opening guns of the spring campaign began to sound along the Rappahannock.

For the past three months the Federal army across the river had had a new commander. Ambrose Burnside had been replaced by General Joseph ("Fighting Joe") Hooker. Having put the army into excellent trim, and having laid the groundwork for a grand offensive operation, Hooker said, "May God have mercy on General Lee, for I will have none!" Hooker had about 135,000 men available for this campaign; Lee had about 60,000.

JOSEPH HOOKER.

Hooker's preliminary moves were good ones. Leaving two corps to demonstrate against Lee at Fredericksburg, he took the rest of his army northwestward along the river. Crossing at a point about twenty miles above Lee's left flank, he circled southeastward to Chancellorsville, arriving there on April 30. This put him about ten miles west of Fredericksburg, or in a position to move against Lee's left rear.

"The enemy," Hooker now told his men, "must either ingloriously fly or . . . give us battle upon our own ground, where certain destruction awaits him."

In spite of the odds, Lee decided to fight. Leaving 10,000 men to face the Federal demonstration at Fredericksburg, he moved the rest of his army westward toward Hooker's main body. Consequently, Hooker's advance troops had barely started eastward from Chancellorsville on

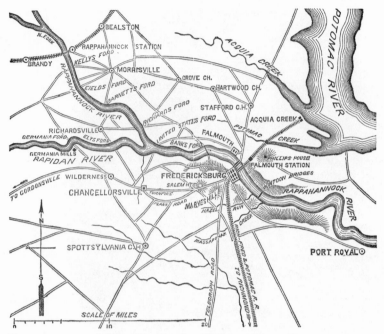

FIELD OF OPERATIONS for Battle of Chancellorsville.

May 1 when they encountered resistance. Says Jackson's aide, James Smith:

How the muskets rattled along a front of a mile or two, across the unfenced fields and through the woodlands! What spirit was imparted to the line, and cheers rolled up along its length, when Jackson and then Lee himself appeared, riding abreast of the line....

Slowly but steadily the line advanced, until at nightfall all Federal pickets and skirmishers were driven back upon the body of Hooker's force at Chancellorsville.

This was no great feat, for "Fighting Joe" had no sooner made contact with Lee and Jackson than he ordered his men to retreat! The remarkable boldness of the Confederate generals in the face of his power, together with his knowledge of their past victories, seemed to turn Hooker's "fight" into "fright." Establishing his army in strong lines at Chancellorsville, he went on the defensive.

That night, with the Confederate soldiers sleeping on their arms, Lee

and Jackson bivouacked near each other, lying on the pine straw in the
woods, Lee covered with his cloak and Jackson with a borrowed cape.
James Smith was on the scene:

Some time after midnight I was awakened by the chill of the
early morning hours, and, turning over, caught a glimpse of a
little flame on the slope above me, and, sitting up to see what it
meant, I saw bending over a scant fire of twigs two men seated
on old cracker boxes and warming their hands over the little
fire. I had to rub my eyes and collect my wits to recognize the
figures of Robert E. Lee and Stonewall Jackson.

The two generals were planning another flank movement. Lee, who had
already split his inferior force (leaving a part of it at Fredericksburg)
was about to split the remainder—an incredibly daring move in the face
of so strong a foe.

The plan called for Lee himself, with 20,000 men, to demonstrate in
Hooker's front as though about to launch a major attack from that
direction. Jackson, meanwhile, was to take about 30,000 men (includ-
ing Stuart's cavalry) on a wide arc to the left and come in on Hooker's
right flank. Jackson's march, which would require the better part of a
day to complete, was to start early in the morning.

In the words of Confederate cavalry officer Fitzhugh Lee:

The sun rose on this eventful 2d of May unclouded and
brilliant. . . . Its rays fell upon the last meeting in this world of
Lee and Jackson. . . . Lee, erect and soldierly, emerged from the
little pine thicket where he had bivouacked during the night,
and stood on its edge . . . to see Jackson's troops file by. When
Jackson came along, he stopped and the two conversed for a
few moments, after which Jackson speedily rejoined his
troops. . . .

Adds Jeb Stuart's chief of staff, Heros von Borcke:

Thus commenced the famous flank march which, more than
any other operation of the war, proved the brilliant strategical
talents of General Lee and the consummate ability of his
lieutenant. . . .

By about four o'clock we had completed our movement . . .
and reached a patch of wood in rear of the enemy's right
wing . . . the 11th corps . . . which was encamped in a large open
field not more than half a mile distant. Halting here, the cavalry
threw forward a body of skirmishers to occupy the enemy's

LAST COUNCIL of Lee and Jackson.

attention while the divisions of Jackson's corps ... moved into line of battle as fast as they arrived.

Ordered to reconnoitre the position of the Federals, I rode cautiously forward through the forest, and reached a point whence I obtained a capital view of the greater part of their troops, whose attitude betokened how totally remote was any suspicion that a numerous host was so near at hand [the sight of the cavalry skirmishers having caused some excitement but no general alarm]. . . .

On my return to the spot where I had left Stuart, I found him, with Jackson and the officers of their respective staffs, stretched out along the grass beneath a gigantic oak, and tranquilly discussing their plans for the impending battle, which both seemed confidently to regard as likely to end in a great and important victory for our arms.

Towards five o'clock Jackson's adjutant ... galloped up to us and reported that the line of battle was formed, and all was in readiness for immediate attack. Accordingly the order was at once given for the whole corps to advance. All hastened forthwith to their appointed posts, General Stuart and his staff joining the cavalry, which was to operate on the left of our infantry.

Scarcely had we got up to our men when the Confederate yell, which always preceded a charge, burst forth along our lines, and Jackson's veterans, who had been with difficulty held back till that moment, bounded forward towards the astounded and perfectly paralyzed enemy, while... our horse artillery [thundered its support]....

The more hotly we [of the cavalry] sought to hasten to the front, the more obstinately did we get entangled in the undergrowth, while our infantry moved on so rapidly that the Federals were already completely routed by the time we had got thoroughly quit of the forest.

It was a strange spectacle that now greeted us. The whole of the 11th corps had broken at the first shock of the attack. Entire regiments had thrown down their arms, which were lying in regular lines on the ground.... Suppers just prepared had been abandoned. Tents, baggage, wagons, cannons, half-slaughtered oxen [abandoned by the regimental butchers], covered the foreground in chaotic confusion, while in the background a host of many thousand Yankees were discerned scampering for their lives as fast as their limbs could carry them, closely followed by our men, who were taking prisoners by the hundreds, and scarcely firing a shot....

Meanwhile a large part of the Federal army, roused by the firing and the alarming reports from the rear, hastened to the field of action and exerted themselves... to arrest the disgraceful rout of their comrades of the 11th corps. Numerous batteries having now joined the conflict, a terrific cannonade roared along the lines, and the fury of the battle was soon at its full height.

One of the staff officers riding with Jackson at this time was Captain R. E. Wilbourn, who relates:

Frequently, during the fiercest of the conflict, he would stop, raise his hand, and turn his eyes toward heaven, as if praying for a blessing on our arms.... Our troops made repeated charges, driving the enemy before them every time, which caused loud and long-continued cheering along our entire line....

I have never seen him seem so well pleased with the progress and results of a fight.... On several occasions ... as he passed the dead bodies of some of our veterans, he halted, raised his hand as if to ask a blessing upon them, and to pray God to save their souls.

Finally the Federals began to hold their ground. At the same time, Jackson's attack was suffering disorganization as the result of its wild sweep.

Stonewall's aide, James Smith, tells what happened next:

Divisions commanders found it more and more difficult as the twilight deepened to hold their broken brigades in hand.... General Jackson ... ordered A. P. Hill's division, his third and reserve line, to be placed in front. While this change was being effected, impatient and anxious, the general rode forward on the turnpike [that led toward Chancellorsville], followed by two or three of his staff and a number of couriers and signal sergeants.

He ... came upon a line of the Federal infantry lying on their arms. Fired at by one or two muskets ... he turned and came back toward his line, upon the side of the road to his left. As he rode near to the Confederate troops, just placed in position and ignorant that he was in the front, the left company began firing ... and two of his party fell from their saddles dead....

Spurring his horse across the road to his right, he was met by a second volley from the right company.... Under this volley ... the general received three balls at the same instant. One penetrated the palm of his right hand.... A second passed around the wrist of the left arm and out through the left hand. A third ball passed through the left arm halfway from shoulder to elbow. The large bone of the upper arm was splintered to the elbow joint, and the wound bled freely.

His horse turned quickly from the fire, through the thick bushes, which swept the cap from the general's head and scratched his forehead, leaving drops of blood to stain his face. As he lost his hold upon the bridle-rein, he reeled from the saddle and was caught by the arms of Captain Wilbourn.... Laid upon the ground, there came at once to his succor General A. P. Hill and members of his staff.

[I] reached his side a minute after, to find General Hill hold-

JACKSON at the moment of his wounding by his own men. His left arm broken and his cap swept off by the brush, he is about to fall from the saddle.

ing the head and shoulders of the wounded chief. Cutting open the coatsleeve from wrist to shoulder, I found the wound in the upper arm, and with my handkerchief I bound the arm above the wound to stem the flow of blood.

Couriers were sent for Dr. Hunter McGuire, the surgeon of the corps and the general's trusted friend, and for an ambulance. Being outside of our lines, it was urgent that he should be moved at once. With difficulty, litter-bearers were brought from the line nearby, and the general was placed upon the litter and carefully raised to the shoulder, I myself bearing one corner.

A moment after, artillery from the Federal side was opened upon us. Great broadsides thundered over the woods. Hissing shells searched the dark thickets through, and shrapnel swept the road along which we moved. Two or three steps farther, and the litter-bearer at my side was struck and fell; but, as the litter turned, Major Watkins Leigh, of Hill's staff, happily caught it.

But the fright of the men was so great that we were obliged to lay the litter and its burden down upon the road. As the litter-bearers ran to the cover of the trees, I threw myself by the general's side and held him firmly to the ground as he attempted to rise. Over us swept the rapid fire of shot and shell, grapeshot striking fire upon the flinty rock of the road all around us, and sweeping from their feet horses and men of the artillery just moved to the front.

Soon the firing veered to the other side of the road, and I sprang to my feet, assisted the general to rise, passed my arm around him, and with the wounded man's weight thrown heavily upon me, we forsook the road. Entering the woods, he sank to the ground from exhaustion; but the litter was soon brought, and again rallying a few men, we essayed to carry him farther, when a second bearer fell at my side.

This time, with none to assist, the litter careened, and the general fell to the ground with a groan of deep pain. Greatly alarmed, I sprang to his head, and, lifting his head as a stray beam of moonlight came through the clouds and leaves, he opened his eyes and wearily said, "Never mind me, Captain; never mind me."

Raising him again to his feet, he was accosted by Brigadier General [William D.] Pender: "Oh, General, I hope you are not seriously wounded. I will have to retire my troops to reform them, they are so much broken by this fire."

But Jackson, rallying his strength, with firm voice said, "You must hold your ground, General Pender. You must hold your ground, sir!" and so uttered his last command on the field.

Again we resorted to the litter, and with difficulty bore it through the bush, and then under a hot fire along the road. Soon an ambulance was reached, and stopping to seek some stimulant at Chancellor's (Dowdall's Tavern); we were found by Dr. McGuire, who at once took charge of the wounded man.

Passing back over the battlefield of the afternoon, we reached . . . the field-hospital of our corps under Dr. Harvey Black. Here we found a tent prepared; and after midnight the left arm was amputated near the shoulder, and a ball taken from the right hand.

All night long it was mine to watch by the sufferer, and keep him warmly wrapped and undisturbed in his sleep. [He had been given chloroform.] At 9 A.M. on the next day, when he aroused, cannon firing again filled the air, and all the Sunday through the fierce battle raged . . . Stuart commanding the Confederates in Jackson's place [and Lee pressing his attack on Hooker's original front]. . . . The long day was passed with bright hopes for the wounded general [and] with tidings of success on the battlefield. . . .

On this day the outnumbered Confederates were busy not only at Chancellorsville, but also on a second front. The Federals who had been left at Fredericksburg crossed the river, bested the town's 10,000 defenders, and came marching along the road from Fredericksburg toward Lee's rear. Remarkably, Lee managed to send enough troops from his Chancellorsville lines to stop the advance.

In the end, the Confederate victory was complete. Demoralized by Lee's audacious tactics and furious assaults, Hooker ordered all units of his great army back across the Rappahannock. He had suffered about 17,000 casualties. Lee's totalled about 13,000.

The Confederate general gave much of the credit for the victory to Jackson. Even while the battle still raged, Lee sent messengers to check on Jackson's condition, telling one of these men: "He has lost his left arm, but I have lost my right." Lee sent his affectionate regards, imploring the wounded general to mend quickly and return to duty.

But Stonewall Jackson—who in the short space of two years had made himself one of the world's immortal soldiers—had fought his final battle. And the Confederate cause was much the worse for this. Chancellorsville was Lee's last great victory. He was one day to say: "If I had had Jackson at Gettysburg, I should have won that battle, and a complete victory there would have resulted in the establishment of the independence of the South."

At first Jackson seemed to be improving, and on Tuesday, May 5, as the Battle of Chancellorsville was ending, he was taken to a comfortable room in a house at Guinea Station, south of Fredericksburg. On Thursday his condition worsened, with pneumonia setting in. That afternoon Mary Anna reached his side, and she was shocked at how he had changed since their last meeting. Her heart was wrung by "his mutilated arm . . . and . . . the desperate pneumonia which was flushing his cheeks, oppressing his breathing, and benumbing his senses."

He rallied when he saw her, and soon said, "My darling, you must cheer up. . . . I love cheerfulness and brightness in a sickroom."

On Friday and Saturday he grew more feverish and more restless, sometimes slipping into delirium. On Sunday morning, says Mary Anna, little Julia was brought in to see him:

. . . although he had almost ceased to notice anything . . . he looked up, his countenance brightened with delight, and . . . he exclaimed, "Little darling! Sweet one!" She was seated on the bed by his side, and after watching her intently, with radiant smiles, for a few moments, he closed his eyes, as if in prayer. . . .

Tears were shed over that dying bed by strong men who were unused to weep, and it was touching to see the genuine grief of his servant, Jim, who nursed him faithfully to the end.

In Dr. McGuire's words:

His exhaustion increased so rapidly that at eleven o'clock Mrs. Jackson knelt by his bed and told him that before the sun went down he would be with his Saviour. He replied, "Oh, no! You are frightened, my child. Death is not so near. I may yet get well."

She fell over upon the bed, weeping bitterly, and told him again that the physicians said that there was no hope. After a moment's pause, he asked her to call me. "Doctor, Anna informs me that you have told her that I am to die today. Is it so?"

When he was answered, he turned his eyes toward the ceiling and gazed for a moment or two as if in intense thought, then replied, "Very good, very good. It is all right." He then tried to comfort his almost heartbroken wife, and told her he had a good deal to say to her, but was too weak. . . .

When told that the whole army was praying for him, he replied, "Thank God. They are very kind." He said, "It is the Lord's day. My wish is fulfilled. I have always desired to die on Sunday."

His mind now began to fail and wander, and he frequently talked as if in command upon the field, giving orders in his old way; then the scene shifted, and he was at the mess table, in conversation with members of his staff; now with his wife and child; now at prayers with his military family.

Occasional intervals of return of his mind would appear, and during one of them I offered him some brandy and water; but he declined it, saying, "It will only delay my departure and do no good; I want to preserve my mind, if possible, to the last."

About half-past one he was told that he had but two hours to live, and he answered again, feebly but firmly, "Very good; it is all right."

A few moments before he died he cried out in his delirium, "Order A. P. Hill to prepare for action! Pass the infantry to the

Jackson's grave at Lexington, Virginia.

front rapidly. Tell Major Hawks—" then stopped, leaving the sentence unfinished.

Presently a smile ... spread itself over his pale face, and he said quietly, and with an expression as if of relief, "Let us cross over the river and rest under the shade of the trees."

Bibliography

FOR FURTHER READING

Douglas, Henry Kyd. *I Rode With Stonewall.* Chapel Hill, N.C.: University of North Carolina Press, 1940.

Henderson, G. F. R. *Stonewall Jackson and the American Civil War.* London, New York, Bombay and Calcutta: Longmans, Green, and Co., 1913.

Selby, John. *Stonewall Jackson as Military Commander.* London: B. T. Batsford Ltd.; and Princeton, New Jersey: D. Van Nostrand Company, Inc., 1968.

Tate, Allen. *Stonewall Jackson the Good Soldier.* New York: Minton, Balch & Company, 1928.

QUOTATION SOURCES

Allan, William. *History of the Campaign of Gen. T. J. (Stonewall) Jackson in the Shenandoah Valley of Virginia.* Part II of Southern Historical Society Papers, New Series, No. 5. Richmond, Va.: B. F. Johnson Publishing Co., 1920.

Annals of the War. Philadelphia: The Times Publishing Company, 1879.

Arnold, Thomas Jackson. *Early Life and Letters of General Thomas J. Jackson.* New York, Chicago, Toronto, London and Edinburgh: Fleming H. Revell Company, 1916.

Battles and Leaders of the Civil War. 4 vols. Robert Underwood Johnson and Clarence Clough Buel (eds.) New York: The Century Co., 1884–1888.

Caldwell, J. F. J. *The History of a Brigade of South Carolinians.* Philadelphia: King & Baird, 1866.

Casler, John O. *Four Years in the Stonewall Brigade.* James I. Robertson, Jr. (ed.). Dayton, Ohio: Morningside Bookshop, 1971. Facsimile of 1906 edition.

Cook, Roy Bird. *The Family and Early Life of Stonewall Jackson.* Richmond, Va.: Old Dominion Press, Inc., 1924.

Cooke, John E. *Stonewall Jackson: A Military Biography.* New York: D. Appleton and Company, 1866.

———. *Stonewall Jackson and the Old Stonewall Brigade.* Edited by Richard Barksdale Harwell. Charlottesville, Virginia: University of Virginia Press, 1954.

———. *The Life of Stonewall Jackson.* Reprint of 1863 edition. Freeport, New York: Books for Libraries Press, 1971.

———. *Wearing of the Gray.* New York: E. B. Treat & Co., 1867.

Dabney, Robert L. *Life and Campaigns of Lieut.-Gen. Thomas J. Jackson.* New York: Blelock & Co., 1866.

Doolady, M. *Jefferson Davis and Stonewall Jackson.* Philadelphia: John E. Potter and Company, 1866.

Gordon, John B. *Reminiscences of the Civil War.* New York: Charles Scribner's Sons, 1904.

Jackson, Mary Anna. *Memoirs of Stonewall Jackson.* Louisville, Ky.: The Prentice Press, 1895.

Jones, John B. *A Rebel War Clerk's Diary.* Earl Schenck Miers (ed.). New York: Sagamore Press, Inc., 1958.

Lee, Fitzhugh. *General Lee of the Confederate Army.* London: Chapman and Hall, Ld., 1895.

Maury, Dabney Herndon. *Recollections of a Virginian.* New York: Charles Scribner's Sons, 1894.

McGuire, Hunter. *Address . . . Delivered on 23d Day of June, 1897, at the Virginia Military Institute . . . upon the Occasion of the Inauguration of the Stonewall Jackson Memorial Building.* Lynchburg, Va.: Virginia Military Institute, 1897.

Moore, Frank (ed.). *The Civil War in Song and Story.* New York: P. F. Collier, 1889.

———. *The Rebellion Record.* 12 vols. New York: G. P. Putnam, 1861–1871.

Nichols, G. W. *A Soldier's Story of His Regiment.* Kennesaw, Ga.: Continental Book Company, 1961. Facsimile of 1898 edition.

Oates, William C. *The War Between the Union and the Confederacy.* New York: The Neale Publishing Co., 1905.

Opie, John N. *A Rebel Cavalryman with Lee, Stuart, and Jackson.* Dayton, Ohio: Morningside Bookshop, 1972. Facsimile of 1899 edition.

Owen, William Miller. *In Camp and Battle with the Washington Artillery.* Boston: Ticknor and Company, 1885. Second edition by Pelican Publishing Company, New Orleans, 1964.

Pollard, Edward A. *The Lost Cause.* New York: E. B. Treat & Co., 1866.

Smith, James Power. *With Stonewall Jackson.* Part I of Southern Historical Society Papers, New Series, No. 5. Richmond, Va.: B. F. Johnson Publishing Co., 1920.

Stiles, Robert. *Four Years Under Marse Robert.* New York and Washington: The
    Neale Publishing Company, 1903.
Taylor, Walter H. *Four Years with General Lee.* New York: D. Appleton and
    Company, 1878.
Under Both Flags: A Panorama of the Great Civil War. Chicago: W. S. Reeve
    Publishing Co., 1896.
Von Borcke, Heros. *Memoirs of the Confederate War for Independence.* 2 vols.
    New York: Peter Smith, 1938. Reprint of 1866 edition.

Index